A NEW GENERATION

A NEW GENERATION

American and Catholic

MICHAEL NOVAK

HERDER AND HERDER

1964
HERDER AND HERDER   NEW YORK
232 Madison Avenue, New York 16, N.Y.

282.73
N 856 N

FOR KAREN

CONTENTS

INTRODUCTION

No moral issue facing the people of the United States will be unaffected by the changes occurring among the new generation of Catholics growing up in America. These Catholics, born since 1930, came to their maturity through the pontificates of Pius XII and John XXIII. They experienced in their youth the upheavals of the Second Vatican Council. Catholics are nearly fifty million strong in the United States. If increasing numbers of their young are moved by the passions for justice, freedom, and unity which moved that great good man, John XXIII, the face of America will unavoidably be changed. These young Catholics bear great responsibility for the quality of American life. They are the natural leaders of other Catholics of the world, in the struggle between the forces of man and the forces of technique. The time in which we live is germinative; it is the beginning of an era; small efforts now will have effects for many generations.

The Church has been in the world for some sixty-five generations; no winter is so cold that she cannot look forward to the spring. It is only the temporary misfortune of the present generation of American Catholics that they have been born into a land at a time in which Catholicism has kept itself isolated from the secular world, and has worn one of its most rigid, restrictive, and uncomprehending masks. They have also lived through the days when that mask began to crack. If they show energy, the mask can be shed like the shell of a cocoon.

For five generations, American priests sheltered their flocks from the cold realities of American life, anticipating a better day. The priest represented the Irish immigrants before cultivated and official America. He created surrogate schools, societies, and cultural forces to stand in his parishioners' lives as the "American experience;" America was too hostile, too complacent, too nativist to enter directly. The German pastor built a solid church, a school that would last, a press that would preserve the German language and Catholic culture in this land of "speculators and libertarians." The Slav pastor shared the disesteem which Nordics showed his flock; the Italian cleric ruled in his own domain, only to struggle against the prejudices of those, including Catholics, from the North. Just as American society in general insisted on a single public school system to weld America into a nation, so American Catholics, each group in its national ghetto, stressed loyalty to their one Church. At first they may have shared the nationalistic biases of Europe against each other; but they were united by a defensive loyalty to their Church and a passion to become purely American: casual, free, rich, and uncontroversial.

To some generations it is given to sow, to others to reap.
For the present generation, assuredly, the anticipated better day has come. Loyalty to Church and country now
takes new forms. The cocoon no longer sets the bounds of
life. Apologetics and self-congratulation are no longer the
range of intellectual creativity. The shell is beginning to
fall; the worm is beginning to take wing. The new form of
loyalty is critical and nervous; it seems, at times, excessively
negative, for it is preoccupied with breaking through the
shell rather than with flight. If you ask those of the new
generation exactly what they want, they often cannot say.
They know better what they do not want to be than what
they desire to be; it is just this uncertainty regarding the
future that marks this generation as creative. When the
trend can be more accurately defined, it will already have
been shaped and perhaps have reached its crest. At present,
the signs are rather of dissatisfaction, restlessness, energy,
trial and error, than of accomplishment. There is a heavi-
ness in the air as before a rain.

The two great overriding facts with which the new generation must come to terms are the facts of being Catholic
and of being American. The Church is historical, in the
sense that it changes greatly from culture to culture, time to
time; its great basic truths belong to all men, at all times,
in all cultures. While the American Church has been building buildings and developing materially, it has borrowed
what intellectual and spiritual life it has from European
theoreticians. Irish and Latin traditions color its popular

piety and ecclesiastical spirit; French, German, and Belgian theologians supply its contemporary intellectual stimulation. The latter rather than the former are helpful to the leaders of the new generation; they, more than the former, are aware of the contemporary needs of a groping, advancing, creative Catholic culture in the throes of transition. Popular emotions and spontaneous, inarticulate faith are not enough; neither is a system of law fashioned for other cultures, other times, and not notably creative. The new generation turns spontaneously to Catholic cultures in secular, rather than in Catholic, nations for their inspiration. The habits of mind fomented in the secular nation appear to be the Church's best ally in times of critique and creativity. The leaders at the Second Vatican Council came, mostly, from such lands.

Eight-hundred-thousand American Catholics are presently in college; year by year the body of American Catholics becomes the most educated in the history of the Church. There are not yet enough translators, scholars, thinkers, writers, doers among these thousands. Still, the shape that Catholicism is taking in America is already different from Catholicism in Europe, as American life in general differs from European life. Moreover, the renewal within the Church cuts beneath the cultural forms of recent centuries to restore an earlier simplicity to Catholic life—and this renewal undercuts the example of recent European Catholic life to which American memories turn. The American character is flexible and mobile, and there is great hope that the present renewal in the Church will strike most swiftly and most deeply among the educated Catholics of the United States. On the other hand, many of the American clergy seem too preoccupied with financial and administrative matters, and the general mass of American Catholics too habituated to the inherited popular piety and ecclesiastical spirit, for the renewal to proceed smoothly. The lifetime of the new generation will be one of conflict, even though the conflict be creative.

The opening chapters of this book concentrate upon the present renewal of the Church and the situation of the Church in America. The United States is the creative land of this century; the center of the struggle between the free human spirit and technology is fixed in her daily life. To the generations preceding our own goes great credit for preserving the faith, for building with great sacrifice the schools and churches the new generation inherits, for inculcating order and regularity. If in turning toward other tasks the new generation sometimes seems unappreciative, it is not out of disloyalty or recklessness; it is out of fidelity to new demands. One phase of American Catholic life is at an end; another is beginning. In its eagerness to get on with the future, the new generation is sometimes insufficiently grateful for the past.

The second set of chapters concentrates on education in America. The young people of our land seem, in general, to find their education irrelevant to much of their lives. They differ from past generations of students in possessing more power: they have money, cars, time, and are less subject to authority both in the family and in school. The mass media feed them with such excitement as was once only the stuff of dreams. Their boredom is not that of seeing too little, hearing too little; it is that of having been exposed already to too much. Moreover, current educational theory merely urges them to become "useful members of society," to make a "useful contribution to society." Students do not always feel like being used. It takes a certain amount of "maturity" to submit to being a cog in a machine. Students may look at their fathers' generation and not wish to live like that. If they are not inclined to be beatniks and not inclined to forget themselves in the mad rush for success, they turn most often (it appears) to the private world of affection and romance, placing on romantic love more hopes than it can satisfy. More young people than adults care to notice turn to alcohol; and not with joy, but with boredom.

The roots of this problem are too deep for quick remedies. The young are candid images of the old. The greater majority, even of the idealistic and the hopeful, are caught in the epistemological nightmare that knowledge is power, that man is a knowing animal, that science is the instrument of control over social, political, physical, and psychological phenomena. They end by thinking of themselves, too, as instruments. They feel that subtly, somehow, they are being used. State, corporation, school, parents, even a man's beloved, use him for their needs. Man has fallen from the kingdom of ends to the kingdom of means; he has no value or importance for himself. This is not the way we talk, but it is the way we live: we are evacuating the tradition of the West. There is no swift, easy, or automatic remedy. There is no slogan to propose. Only the arduous work, by which first one man, then another, makes himself into a person and refuses to be only a technician, even a contented technician, can restore man to the kingdom of ends. The enemy of this kingdom is neither science nor the Church. The enemy is the joint army of scientific and ecclesiastical technicians, supported by other bureaucrats as well.

The last chapter, which alone constitutes part three, attempts to clarify the philosophic attitude which governs the entire book. The attitude proposed is empirical and pragmatic, but it seems to be more adequate to the experience of human life than classical empiricism or pragmatism. To put the point more technically than it will be put in that chapter, British empiricism from Hume through Russell, Wittgenstein and Ayer, inclines toward a simplified view of knowing. It tends to overrate the role of sense observation, and to slight intelligent reflection and reflective consciousness. As a consequence, the English tradition is especially inadequate in dealing with the self, the various kinds of self-awareness, and the particular kind of self-knowledge which constitutes a man as a person. On the other hand, American pragmatism from James and Dewey through C. I. Lewis, Morton White, and Willard Quine, also ends by doing less than justice to the human person and his experience of himself. It seems that our traditional respect for the person is not preserved by the insights of philosophers but by certain conditions in American and British life; our philosophy lags behind our living. Thus we must extend empiricism and pragmatism to all the experiences of human consciousness if we wish to fashion a philosophical vehicle for expressing our own beliefs, and to create a transcultural, human philosophy. Such an empiricism seems also to be the most adequate philosophy for expressing the relation of Christian faith to life.

Moreover, such an empiricism or pragmatism has strong reverberations in tradition—if not since the fourteenth century, certainly in the attachment of Aquinas to Aristotle. Latin Scholasticism missed the point of that attachment, and, largely, removed the empirical and pragmatic elements from Scholastic methodology. This is why Latin Scholasticism seems so far removed from reality, and why it was fair game, in the seventeenth century, for Locke and the empiricists on one hand, and for Descartes on the other. Those who are interested in joining hands with the best in the ancient tradition may find that study which proceeds by way of contemporary empiricism and pragmatism will be at least as fruitful as the study of Latin Scholasticism, and certainly no more misleading. The discussion of these points in part three is not technical; it proceeds rather by trying to convey, from several different approaches and from different angles, an attitude or epistemological stance.

In order to work out his position thoroughly, a philosopher must not fear to enter many other fields. He is by no means a professional in all the details and methods of these other fields; his special competence is with questions of point of view. Throughout, I have tried to employ a consistent point of view, empirical, pragmatic, realistic, and Christian, and to compare it with other points of view, in the consideration of a number of contemporary problems. The solution of these problems is crucial for what it means to be an American and a Catholic in the present generation.

PART ONE

A NEW GENERATION

1 THE RENEWAL

Two generations before the present one, Pope Leo XIII stirred the deeps of the Catholic Church. Many thinkers and laborers had prepared the way for Leo; many others began the long task of carrying his reforms into effect. A thick crust had formed on the Church over the centuries, massive walls had been put up, blocking off the freedom of the Church and inhibiting her movement: walls of isolation, defense, fear. Above all, the Church has seemed to be afraid of her own gift: freedom. The effort of Leo XIII to reform the Church, therefore, was a peculiar kind of revolution. In the words of Emmet John Hughes, "It struck not at the core of old principles—but at the crust around them. It rebelled not at the cherishing of venerable precepts—but at their blurring." There has been much to reform in the life of the Church, but, by the nature of the case, those in positions of authority under the pope were not always the ones able to see what was amiss. In their very efforts to preserve order, they served the older order. The Second Vatican Council began to show the Church the way to a new order, through orderly renewal.

Meanwhile, as the Church has begun to have a taste of new reform, so Protestants have begun to have a taste of the "Catholic" experience. In establishing the World Council of Churches, they have begun to live under the pressures of catholicity. For this reason, Catholics in our generation can appreciate some things in their own Church by looking at it as Protestants do, and Protestants can learn about themselves in reflecting on their new international, communal experience. The World Council has come to know the conflicts between East and West, Latin and Nordic, American and Asian. It has tried to reconcile the freer tendencies of the sects with the formal tendencies of the churches. It has felt the centripetal and centrifugal forces of individualism and the sense of community. The sheer administrative task of coordination and planning, together with the inevitable bureaucratic compromises of an international body, disconcert, perplex, and weary young idealists. The World Council tends to become a worldly council.

Roman Catholics have lived with such developments for so long that they are accustomed to them, and are seldom so swiftly disheartened as some young Protestants seem to be —after the complex, mammoth meeting in New Delhi in 1961, for example. Catholics are sometimes so docile to the inevitability of bureaucracy that they do nothing to oppose it. On the other hand, they have long been at work on a philosophy of institutional life to keep the bureaucratic and the prophetic in tension. Catholic inner life has long been attuned to the jading realities of human institutions, as well as to the comfortable familiarity they bring. Their faith is that God, nevertheless, humbled Himself to the use of human means, accepting labors in the human manner even where divine effects are at stake. Their most adequate philosophy takes a position above the counterpositions of classical rationalism and empiricism; all the following chapters will be trying to articulate its nature and methods. This philosophy stands on its own merits; and the faith, too, stands on its own merits—not all who believe must be philosophers. But it happens that without philosophy, the faith cannot be articulated in thought or even in action; and while there may be many philosophies to help articulate the riches of faith, by their fruits some may be seen to be more adequate than others.

To understand the present renewal in Roman Catholicism, then, it is necessary to understand the role of institutional action, the law, and external forms, in aiding liberty and unity in the life of the spirit. It is important to find an adequate philosophical starting place. Body and spirit and those things which pertain to each, for example, are not to be conceived as two antagonistic, separate factors; they are not to be pictured as prisoner in prison house, or as a ghost in a machine. Christianity is incarnational, redeeming the flesh, promising resurrection to the flesh. The Protestant genius (even in Kant, for example) seems to favor purity; the Catholic, to favor the human. In this seem to lie the opposite cultural weaknesses of the two parties—except in

America, where Catholics have taken over the Puritan attitude toward the flesh and the world. In themselves, the
humble demands of the flesh are not scandalous; but they
require watching. To understand Catholicism, the Protestant must allow his mind and heart to move in the direction
of the human. To understand Protestantism, the Catholic
must move in the direction of the prophetic.

From the human machinery of an external church to the
use of pictures, statues, mementoes, the Roman Catholic
is accustomed to lifting up his heart with the aid of what
his eyes can see, his ears hear, his fingers touch. When the
human aid is deformed, ugly, even misleading, as it often is,
he recalls Isaiah 53: "Forgotten and as it were the most
abject of men . . . no comeliness, no beauty in Him. . . ."
and turns his heart to the cross where Jesus does not look
like God.

The trouble with institutions is, however, that the individual feels he will be crushed—and he often is. If man
were not a social animal, the usefulness of institutions could
be denied at once. But no matter how man turns or twists,
he keeps coming back to institutional forms of expression
and decision. The seat of religion—of God's Presence—is
within, unseen, in the inner heart; but that seed cannot
help bearing fruit, branching outward into the sky where
men can see it. The planting of that seed, the tending of
that seed, needs laborers, and they are not too many but too
few. Thus the laws of individual life become subsumed in
the laws of organic, societal life. In this subsumption lie

many grievous pains, conflicts, and as many tragedies as
purifications; Christ Himself died at the hands of the
religious institution.

The individual is apt to believe that the Gospels should
come and be realized at once, that he in his person is the
judge and arbiter of history; and, in a sense—but no simple
sense—he is. He is also a single individual in the long march
of the People of God through history, not until the end of
which will the full growth and stature of Jesus Christ be
achieved, not until the end of which will the kingdom of
Justice and Love, of Truth and Peace, be realized. The
Gospels, then, are not now in their perfect state, nor are
they meant to be. Nor is the individual to find a perfect,
pure world. The Christian is not called to see the Gospels
fructify before his eyes; Christ did not.

The labor to transform history is a communal one. It has
its ups and downs, its cycles of fervor and change. What
brings about a rising cycle of renewal? It is not an isolated
man. It may be a single man, who by personal command
and God's grace moves many others—a Paul, a Luther, a
Wesley.[1] But it can only be a man acting through an insti-

[1] Some Catholics would object to listing Luther and Wesley as
bearers of grace, because they have introduced disunity into the
Body of Christ. But three centuries later, grace can be seen operating among the children of Luther and Wesley: "By their fruits
you shall know them." Protestant and Catholic must leave judgment of each other to God, even while each holds his own convictions, even while each labors without ceasing for the unity which
both desire.

tution, an institution which reaches out to others, and supplies by preaching, education, cultural discipline, the atmosphere in which the words of revelation are given their sense. Cold print in books, repeated words in speech, mean nothing without cultural referents. It is all important to understand, in any given institution (United States Congress, United Nations, a Christian church) what are the avenues by which change can be introduced into the intellectual-imaginative context of the moment; what are the roads of influence by which renewal is brought about. Insights that serve to explain individual renewal are not sufficient; institutions are not nearly so simple and direct— ardently motivated individuals easily cancel one another out.

The command of Genesis was: "Increase, multiply, and possess the earth." Thanks largely to scientific technique, and to the intellectual bent of Christianity (cherishing as no other world religion does an incarnational and progressive view of history), the fulfillment of that command has been made possible. In our day, men are filling the earth and, pressing together, beginning to think similar thoughts, read of the same events, see the same photos, suffer from the same disasters. We are entering what Teilhard de Chardin has called in The Phenomenon of Man the "noosphere" of the evolutionary process: the spiritual unification of men heretofore spread around the world in isolation. It is inevitable that we think in corporate terms: we are one body, branches of one vine. An analysis of the experiences of Roman Catholicism, an institution whose sense of the corporate nature of man has managed to endure, cannot be a disadvantage, even to non–Catholics, as we move toward the religious forms of tomorrow.

As it would be an inexcusable waste if Protestants simply abandoned, without learning from, the institution they set out to reform, so it would be tragic if Catholicism, the body needing reform, did not learn from the reformers. Hans Küng, in his *The Council, Reform, and Reunion*, has not been easy on either party. To understand present-day Roman Catholicism, it is necessary to grasp the fact that the Reformation happened; that the cultural and social movements it started have affected the human conscience to its roots. The conscience of Christianity is not now the same as it was in 1617, or even in 1917. Nor can a young Catholic in America, for example, grow up without thinking of liberty of conscience, of individual judgment, differently than did his ancestors of 1617 or his family of 1917. His next-door neighbors have been friendly Protestants; he's heard Protestant ministers on the radio; in the public schools and secular colleges (over half the Catholic students attend these) it is Protestant, not Catholic, Christianity he is likely to encounter. But the more deeply cutting factor is that the intellectual movements generated by Protestantism, Kant's ethic, v.g., or the very different ethics of Locke and Mill, are main presuppositions of the modern world. The words "free man," self-determination," "liberty of conscience," "separation of church and state," have in our consciousness a Protestant rather than a Catholic ring; few in our culture would, or could, remove the association. The Catholic of our generation is—by virtue of the very air he breathes—indebted to the Protestant inheritance; he too benefits (not, though as if all has been gain) by gains won seemingly in the teeth of his own inheritance. Many Catholics, no doubt, would call this an imbibing of toxins; and surely like all the blessings of human history it is not unmixed—not all that Protestantism has brought with it is good. But there is clearly, and inevitably, a Catholic conscience now, quite different from that of the Catholic generations closer to peasant, paternalistic Europe. Intellectually, this conscience finds its best expression in Europe, in men like Küng, Geiselmann, Rahner, Daniélou, and others. But on a wide cultural basis, the millions of Catholic college graduates of the United States—the most sophisticated, religiously educated laity the church has ever known —will one day prove a more important voice.

There are two major tools to be used in an analysis of Roman Catholicism as an institution. One is a grasp of its national differences; the other is a grasp of the various roles within it. As for national differences, it will surprise nobody that there are "kinds" of Catholic conscience. "Surrounded with variety," the Psalm chants of the Beloved. The Italian conscience is so far different from the Irish conscience on such things as sexual love, for example, that comparison can only be mirthful. Not that the commandment of God changes, only that emphases, fears, attitudes, inhibitions spur individual consciences to very different reactions. The Irish worry about vanishing, the Italians about finding more room. James Joyce was banned in Catholic Ireland and the Protestant United States; Dante puts the unchaste in the highest, least serious circle of hell. The American Catholic conscience, as I have hinted, leans rather to Irish than to Italian precedents, to the Gospels' good or ill.

There are national differences in paternalism, too. Where the people are not educated, the clergy fulfill many roles at once: religious, social, cultural and perhaps political as well. As the culture becomes more complex and diversified, laymen grow up into these roles one by one, though in their struggle to assume them, clericalism and anticlericalism are often generated for a time. Today, in several developed nations, the Church is beginning to feel the blossoming of an educated, articulate laity, itself repository of the Faith, itself witness and voice. Finally, there are national differences in cultural experience and in what Maritain calls "styles" of holiness. The inner-directed, somber religious type has no monopoly on the Gospels; the easy-going, affable, outer-directed American witnesses to a freshness, charity, and tolerance that have a glory of their own to give to God.

One of the deficits in a pluralistic society is that no one individual sees or understands the whole; each speaks, deprecatingly at that, from his own partial point of view. The businessman condemns the professor; the man of the academy comes to believe that he speaks for disinterested truth (from the point of view of his own discipline, of course); the artist nonconforms; the millworker believes himself realistic and "down-to-earth;" the clergyman knows how God would want things done. In Roman Catholicism, there are likewise different, often conflicting, points of view related to the six major institutional roles. No doubt such points of view are only occupational hazards; faithfulness to the Gospels necessitates transcending them. But we may safely say that, on the average, men rise but little, and fit-fully, above their given role. Renewal in Roman Catholi-cism depends upon its penetration of each of these roles.

The arrowtip of Roman Catholic leadership is, of course, the Holy Father. He is the servant of the servants of Christ. By the gift of the Holy Spirit given the Church, and for the sake of the Church, under stringent conditions, explicitly defined and rarely fulfilled, the Pope transcends his own personal limitations and speaks for the whole Church. Otherwise, he is a fallible leader, more or less adequate to his task: which is to act as Catholics believe Peter did, as a center of unity and of crystallization of conscience. It should also be remarked that even his infallible, *ex cathedra* statements are not frozen footprints, fixed and never chang-ing, but rather gradations on scale of clarification, repre-senting the Church's best understanding of its faith at any given time. In later times, as more is understood, it is to be expected that the earlier consciousness will receive comple-mentary and fuller, modifying lights. Most statements of Roman faith are worded in the negative: (as it were)

"This is *not* what we believe. . . ." or: "If anyone believes this . . . he is outside our communion." Precisions about the positive content of faith are most frequently left open.

Secondly, there are the bishops. If the Pope is the arrow-tip, they are the arrowhead. As the collective successors of the apostles, they too share in the power of speaking for the whole Church, transcending (when they speak in concert) their individual and collective weaknesses. Just how Catholics understand their faith in the power and infallibility of the bishops is not yet clear. At the second session of the Second Vatican Council, the assembled Council Fathers voted by overwhelming majorities, in the famous votes of October 30, 1963, to direct the theological commission to prepare a strong, specified statement on the matter. If a good text is forthcoming at a later session, perhaps the Council will find it ripe for ratification, thus complementing and modifying the statement of the First Vatican Council in 1870 about the role of the pope. Meanwhile, in his own diocese, the bishop is supreme. He is the shepherd, and in him and his flock the traditional faith has its local testimony. Thus, Roman Catholicism is seriously decentralized; and every effort at renewal must cope with the independence and diversity of the many hundred bishops of the world.

Thirdly, renewal must cope with the Roman Curia. The Curia is the civil service of the Church, centered in Rome, staffed chiefly but not entirely by Italian priests, monsignori and a few laymen, and divided into approximately a dozen commissions over each of which a cardinal presides. The Curia is a career service; young men generally enter it from their seminary days on, but, of course, newcomers join the ranks at all stages. The central position of the Curia gives it a vocal, public role in the Church disproportionate to its limited composition; its guidance of universities, seminaries and doctrinal discussions gives it a stronger grip over the *ésprit* of the Church than its range of vision warrants. The Curia is not the Church, only an administrative, bureaucratic servant of the Church. There are many, and not least many bishops, who hope urgently for the internationalization of the Curia, the modification of its powers, or the creation of an international council to assume some of its tasks. Pope Paul himself urged precisely such reforms on September 21, 1963, and many other voices took them up in later meetings of the second session of the Council. It has happened too often that when, after much effort, someone has succeeded in nursing a little flame to life, curial Rome has insensitively smothered it with ash.

Fourthly, there are the clergy—technically only the priests, but also the Sisters and Brothers. These are they who live as eunuchs in the world, for the kingdom of God's sake; whose affections and labors go solely for that kingdom. By their renouncing of ordinary life in the world, the clergy have a role clearly distinct from that of the layman. It is not surprising that they have, too, an ecclesiastical, clerical outlook. The factors involved in the cleric's personal identification of himself with his office, and in his resistance or openness to change or criticism in that role, are crucial for renewal. It is the ordinary parish priest, the Sister or Brother in the classroom, who is the official Christ-figure for the local people. Grass-roots renewal must get to the clergy and religious; and to the inquisitive and alive among them, it is.

Fifthly and sixthly, there are two groups of laymen. I would like to divide them into the prophetic and the non-prophetic, the good who can and do speak out their faith, and those who do not. But in our overanalytical society, it seems to occur more and more frequently that those with the penetrating, critical vision have very little of agape's fire in their own lives; they formulate, but they do not live; they are only para-prophets. For this reason, I choose education or, better, the ability to reflect and to articulate, rather than prophecy as the distinguishing line between these two groups of laymen.

All laymen belong to the *hearing church*, to whom instruction comes from the *teaching church*, the ordained ministers. But the hearing church must testify, too, to what it hears, and to the faith that is in it. It, too, as Newman saw, has an as yet undefined role to play in the elucidation of faith in the Church's consciousness. The faith lives in the people; but what is it they believe? They need spokesmen, just as they need the humble holy ones who live the faith fully although never able to verbalize it. These two groups, intellectuals and humble ones, need each other; and the Church without them is top-heavy and officious.

To read the history of the Church—at whatever period,

from the purportedly smooth and fervent early generations to the present—is a sobering lesson in human mediocrity, heroism, and evil. Yet few generations have known the ferment and grace of our own; it is, perhaps, the blood of our century's dead or imprisoned that wins this life for us. Roman Catholicism has been blessed for nearly a hundred years with pontiffs of unusual energy, vision, and holiness of life. The tearing of the Papal States from their hands seems to have acted, rather, as the tearing of fetters from their feet. The papacy has been much purified by the change. Correspondingly, beginning with the pontificate of Leo XIII in 1878, a series of urgent directives have come from the popes in the form of encyclicals addressed to all the bishops, priests, and faithful of the world. From Leo's *Immortale Dei* on modern states and *Rerum novarum* on the need for a reconstruction of the socioeconomic order, to Pius XI's *Casti connubii* on the family and marriage and *Quadragesimo Anno* again on the social order, to Pius XII's *Mediator Dei* on the liturgy and *Divino Afflante Spiritu* on renewal of Scripture studies, to John XXIII's *Mater et Magistra* and *Pacem in terris*, an amazing stream of reflection, criticism, encouragement, and command has been injected into the body of the Church. It is as though, their role made clear by the struggles of the nineteenth century, the popes have been able to seize on their vocations with extraordinary intelligence and vigor.

Too seldom finding support among the intermediate clergy or in the Curia, the popes seem to have allied themselves, further, with the resurgent Catholic intellectual life of all Europe but especially of the Northern countries. The popes have been called "liberal popes" and these intellectuals have been called "liberal Catholics," because for different reasons and with different criteria they often joined the liberal battles of our time. Their leading cry has been against the suffocating of the Church by the bourgeois mentality. Religion is not individualistic piety, practiced at night prayers and on Sunday, a sweetmeat on the bread of a rugged bourgeois morality; religion cares very little for the conventions of the middle classes. Through religion, justice and charity are to enter every cranny of the world: yeast to leaven the whole. From top to bottom, life must enter the world, breaking apart the starch-collared, complacent forms of a dying civilization.

An early prophet of this intellectual resurgence was not a believer: Henri Bergson, who by his lectures at the Sorbonne freed a coterie of young thinkers from the small view of positivism. Léon Bloy, Charles Péguy ("The Father of Modern Catholicism"), Jacques and Raïssa Maritain, Georges Rouault, Ernest Psichari; then Paul Claudel, Gabriel Marcel, François Mauriac, Antoine St. Exupéry, Georges Bernanos; the priests: Clerissac, Daniélou, De Lubac, Mounier, Chardin, Sertillanges and others; and the young saint, Thérèse of Lisieux (1873-1897), who became patroness of France co-equal with Joan of Arc, were (and are) leading figures in this Renaissance. In Scandinavia, Sigrid Undset; in Germany, Romano Guardini, Josef

Pieper, Gertrude von le Fort, Edith Stein, and (if one may count her) Simone Weil; in Spain, José Gironella; in England, Newman, Hopkins, Chesterton, Belloc, Waugh, Green, Knox, Dawson, Barbara Ward and others; in Italy, Don Sturzo, De Gaspari, and Fanfani (whose graduate thesis *Protestantism, Catholicism, and Capitalism* stands beside Max Weber's classic)—all over Europe intelligent and deeply Catholic voices began to be heard. These are the nearest ancestors of the new generation. What seemed after the French Revolution to be dying to ash—schools and universities confiscated, little left but cloistered seminaries in which Catholic intelligence might retire to lick its wounds —came to life in an efflorescence of creative achievement which is not in full flower yet.

It is true, however, that the administrative-minded, whether curial, episcopal, sacerdotal, religious or lay, still are discomfited by this resurgence. Among the young, there is less resistance to change; but the resistance is not basically one of age. It is rather, affecting all to some degree, the burden of the flesh of incarnation. Ministers of grace become administrators, canon law takes up more thought than the Gospels, the smooth functioning of the machine becomes more important than the extraordinary individual. "It is hard enough to keep things together the way they are, without trying every new idea that comes along; the received law is plain, the requirements for salvation are simple, people have got along splendidly for years this way," the nonprophetic will say. "Those who will be saved will be saved, and those who won't, won't." Workers who have borne the heat of the day know that God is a patient God, and that life, no matter what the effort, continues along pretty much on an average. In short, renewal is not an idea favored by the administrative mind, except rhetorically. It doesn't matter that the popes insist upon it, time and again, in countless forms, in every avenue. "The Pope be damned," it would be replied, if propriety allowed.

No one accident did so much harm to the Catholic renewal, before the Council, as the epithet "liberal" affixed to its leaders. Far from flirting with the current of thought generated by the Enlightenment and the social-intellectual thinking of the avant-garde nonbeliever, these leaders are those most active in striving to regain the Catholic tradition. It is they who are doing the researches in Scripture, in archeology, in the Fathers, in early Greek and Hebrew as well as Latin theology, in historic Christian culture, in personalist economics and sociology, in nonrationalistic philosophy, in the neglected fields of Christian sensibility and Christian imagination—they who look upon themselves as returning to tradition. It occurs too frequently, on the contrary, that those who differ with them cite as *their* tradition what hardly dates earlier than the sixteenth century: Trent in theology, Bentham in economics.

But it is not name-calling that is important; neither is it the fruitful grappling and struggling of day-to-day dialectic. What counts is that at many places in Catholicism the breath of the Spirit is felt moving: congregations are saying the dialogue Mass; tentative gropings in church architecture have begun; a fresh body of literature, of philosophy, of theology, is already larger than a man can manage; lay orders and secular institutes have sprung up as new concepts of evangelical life in the world. The Second Vatican Council is carrying this ferment into the very center of the Church.

The story of the Catholic renewal may be told in even shorter form: Catholicism deeply misses those who were among its most zealous and prophetic sons, those who represented in her the energy of reform. Their loss was to her the great tragedy of the Reformation, the loss within herself of much of the tension between prophecy and ministry. It has taken long to build that tension again.

Meanwhile, how does the renewal fare in America?

"The Church," a friend of mine parodies Clemenceau, "is much too valuable to entrust to the clergy." An increasing number of educated American Catholic laymen, in proportion as they penetrate more deeply into their faith, are beginning to share that sentiment. In fact, the hopes for a prophetic Catholicism in America seem to rest chiefly with the laity. Far too much control is exercised over individual priests and religious, no matter how alert and creative, for new directions to be expected often from them. As low-ranking officers in the army must get "clearance" before publishing their views, so must priests. Army discipline applied to priests has advantages for regularity; freedom, creativity, and public discussion suffer.

But the difficulty is that American Catholics are extremely deferential to their clergy; it is hard for them to take initiative or, once having taken it, to fight against clerical opposition. More vocal than in Ireland or Spain, American Catholic laymen are nevertheless quiet and respectful compared to others in the Church's history. Dante, figuratively, sent popes to hell. Chaucer drew an exquisitely damning portrait of his cultivated prioress, not to mention what he did to pardoner and monks. "Clerics . . . have much in the mouth," William Langland wrote in *Piers Plowman*; and he complained poignantly that they were as removed from Christ as others in the realm. Often in ecclesiastical history the wielders of tart critical tongues (Catherine of Siena) and upholders of individual conscience (Joan of Arc) show up some time after their death on the calendar of saints.

Closer to our own time, the searing and almost unprintable language of Léon Bloy shattered many a sweet-faced plaster statue in bourgeois France, and freed for many young people—among them Georges Rouault, the Maritains, Mauriac and Claudel—the harsh, pure spirit of prophecy. In *The Diary of a Country Priest*, Georges Bernanos wrote: "The word of God is a red-hot iron. . . . Comforting truths, they call it! . . . Why, the priest who descends the pulpit of Truth, with a mouth like a hen's vent, a little hot but pleased with himself, he's not been preaching: at best he's been purring like a tabbycat." In a much more gentlemanly fashion—but he was an Englishman—the eminent Newman is said to have risen for a toast, at a banquet upon his reception of the cardinal's hat, and to have said quietly: "To conscience. And to the Pope."

Many believers and unbelievers alike make faith a blind affair. For them, in matters concerning freedom–authority, intelligence–faith, there is no *both/and*; everything is *either/or*. For professional anti-Catholics, religious authority is as clear as Hitler's Reich, and I am afraid that for some believers it is also that clear, though infinitely more benevolent, limited in scope, and moral rather than physical. Professor Zahn's new book German Catholics and Hitler's War suggests the complexity: where individual conscience has no voice against authority, the Gospels suffer. For the Catholic, individual conscience and the authority of the Church are both indispensable.

But as in other institutions the nonofficial power easily becomes a mere formality. In the liturgy for the ordination of a priest, for example, the bishop exhorts the laity to help him decide whether the young men are worthy. "As the judgment of one person, or even of several, may be affected and misled by favor and partiality, it is well to ascertain the general opinion. . . . If then anyone has aught to their prejudice, for God's sake and in God's name let him boldly come forward and speak. . . ." Yet this exhortation is no longer acted upon; it is the record of a much more plain straightforward faith (500–700 A.D.).

There are wide extremes even among intelligent Catholics on the role of clerical authority. In the last century, W. G. Ward, one of the most active agitators on the issue of papal infallibility, is reported to have desired nothing more than to find a new papal encyclical waiting for him every morning at breakfast. The taste of other Catholics runs to different breakfast reading. The Catholics at the National Review hadn't minded papal thinking, and had even rather suggested that they represented the leading edge of traditional religious thinking in the West, but with their flippant "Mater si, Magistra no!" they became independent. The point is that there is no "Catholic view" which a free, independent journal run by laymen has to follow. (An official organ of a bishop is another matter.) The competence of a journal of public affairs lies in the realm of this world and its concerns, and that realm is uniquely the layman's.

What does this realm include? The world is not divided into sacred and profane—one part religion and the rest secular; such a division effectively removes religion from life. Christian life is not icing on a cake; it is yeast in bread. However, all life is not to be subordinated to clerical judgment, nor is a "kingdom of God" to be built on earth. This is the temptation of the Grand Inquisitor and religious idealists generally; it is an effort to fix religion in a social system, to mass-produce saints, to put God in human hands, at the bidding of human methods. The naïve medieval solution was doomed for all its hopes to fall prey to Machiavellians.

The crucial question is how far the Gospels can be realized in present conditions. How, most safely—both for the Gospels and for men? The realities of any moment allow only so much of the ideal to be realized. Segregation is clearly against Christian conscience. Yet some bishops tolerate abuse while others wield excommunication. Laymen have an indispensable role to play in these debates, for they are experts in estimating "present conditions." In proportion as an issue requires judgment of present conditions rather than of doctrine, the layman's competence and authority grows. Thomas à Becket was admirable for his opposition to Henry II; the bishops of Puerto Rico entered a trickier realm in 1960. Their vocation entails speaking out on the Gospels at whatever cost in popularity; but a democracy has its own rules and these they did not observe.

Generally, the Latin countries and Ireland lean heavily toward paternalism in Church affairs. It may be significant that these societies are largely agricultural and poor. From the point of view of the nonbelieving liberal, there is a causal connection between their Catholicism and their backwardness. From the point of view of their local clergy, there is a connection between the "material" progress of the industrial countries and their Protestantism and secularism. It is from these two points of view that the image of a feudal, obscurantist Church versus the aggressive march of time draws continued sustenance. But it is long since out of date. The Catholic spirit of France, Germany and the Lowlands, for example, is a great deal more independent and creative than in the poorer Mediterranean countries. Somewhat ironically, the last 75 years have witnessed an alliance between lay intellectuals and "liberal popes," in which both have often had to go over the heads of the intermediate clergy.

Pius XI sadly admitted that the tragedy of the nineteenth century for the Church was the loss of the working classes. In *Rerum novarum*, his own manifesto on the social order, conceived with the help of vigorous Catholic intellectuals in the north, Leo XIII urged a new relationship of the Gospels and the world. Leo's fundamental notion was that human society is called to grow up into the idealism of the Gospels—a social order of freedom, justice, and love. *Rerum novarum* turned Catholicism away from the individualistic piety of "saving one's soul" to the larger task of realizing the Gospels in all aspects of personal, social, and institutional life. The method was not to be by fiat from above, but organically, by Christians living as Christians in their lay tasks. Catholicism, therefore, became a revolutionary moral force vis-à-vis bourgeois society—the society which nourishes the anesthetized Christianity which Nietzsche reviled. In practice, of course, the innate conservatism of the Church as an institution has often prevailed, and many Catholics furiously resist the "new things" Leo announced.

What effect the coming of industrialization and democracy is going to have on the Italian clergy, or what the influx of tourists, students, and foreign books will do in Spain, is still unclear. But it seemed quite certain on the eve of the Second Vatican Council, that the clergy from nondemocratic, nonindustrial societies quite outnumbered the more liberal clergy of the north. Of more than 230 American bishops, most seemed to have been prevented by the immigrant ghettos from having grasped the impact of the American experience; they seemed largely to think with the Italians. Perhaps this is because so many of them are canon lawyers and administrators, trained in Rome, and a little overawed at having risen from the ranks of the American lower middle class to their high posts in the international Church. (There are, of course, important exceptions, especially among the younger priests.)

Some of the national differences came out clearly in the months before the Council. Hans Küng's *The Council, Reform and Reunion* is as scathing a critique of the life of the Church as our generation has seen; two cardinals—one Austrian, one French—contributed forewords. In Italy, a not wholly dissimilar effort by the Jesuit, Riccardo Lombardi, was publicly censured in the official *Osservatore Romano*, and withdrawn from circulation. In the United States infinitely lesser rumblings won cautions from the Apostolic Delegate, charges of "insolence" from a bishop in New Jersey, and admonitions from a bishop in California (names unnamed, articles uncited).

American Catholics have a deep and in some ways admirable respect for their clergy. In the first place, in the struggles of immigration and adaptation, the clergy kept them together. In the second place, the American clergy have at least until recently been without much influence within the Establishment, and so have been far more on the side of the laboring man and the unions than their European counterparts. The intercession of Cardinal Gibbons and Archbishop Ireland in Rome figured prominently in Leo XIII's defense of the working man in *Rerum novarum*. Again, American Catholics are drawn largely from

European peasant stock, and they brought the peasant's reverence for God's ministers with them to the American cities. There, American nativist prejudice threw priest and parishioner together, whereas in Europe the struggles of the proletariat and the very poor often separated the European Catholic from his clergy. In Rome, little boys sometimes shout "*Cockroaches! Parasites!*" to clerics they pass in the street; in America, on the other hand, they grow red in the face, bow, or duck, and say: "Good afternoon, Father."

This American respect for the clergy can be an Achilles heel, however. For if the layman is not active, critical, and creative, a great deal of energy and talent is lost to the Church. The trouble is, the older generations—both clerical and lay—thought of the Church as pretty much clerical. The layman sat and listened, and dipped his hand into his pocket. Father did the rest. And what Father didn't do, Sister did in the parochial school. Parents largely abdicated their responsibility for the religious education of their children to the Sisters. (Archbishop Ireland insisted, in the last century, that a parochial school system was a mistake; that Catholics in the public schools would do more good for both Catholicism and for America than a separate school system. The other view prevailed.)

It is not only the shelter of parochial school education, but also the Sunday sermons or, more often, the exhortations and admonitions of the home, that constitute the American Catholic ghetto. The ethos of a group on the defensive is "preserve the faith," "stick together," "listen

to your elders," "cause no scandal," "learn to be prudent."
The educated layman must soon outgrow this outlook, and
the accompanying clerical world view derived from a seminary course duly memorized or a smattering of theology given
the nuns; and in his growth he faces crises. His scarred emotions may not let him see clearly afterward; a whole host of
American artists—Eugene O'Neill, Hemingway, O'Hara,
Farrell, Fitzgerald, Katherine Anne Porter, Mary McCarthy,
John Ciardi—broke with their Catholic past (some shaped
by it more than others). Many of the talented who did not
leave the faith have bitter memories of dull, basically insecure authorities.

The layman knows that the Catholic ghetto has shaped
most of the clergy and that the world of the universities and
the journals is not familiar to them. Again, the layman
realizes that fear and insecurity are at work in the ethos of
the ghetto and, naturally enough, among those raised suddenly from the ranks to high places. Before the Council, any
creative or critical movement seemed to the safety-conscious
a "stepping out of bounds," "unheard of," and even a "betrayal." Nevertheless, it is very difficult for Catholic intellectuals, looking around at what can be said and done in France
and Germany, to understand why American bishops should
actually lag *behind* what is permitted. Despite papal permission for afternoon masses, for example, and directives to
encourage lay participation in the liturgy, some bishops
simply are inert and their dioceses do not share these benefits. What outsiders call a well-heeled, monolithic organiza-

tion looks to insiders like a clumsy, complicated, power-fragmented body, marvelously subject to obstruction.

The Catholic layman can, however, pursue his own studies and writing, without the clergy ever taking note of him. He is not "official;" he speaks only for himself—unlike the poor priest who, whether he wishes it or not, is taken as speaking for the whole Church. (The point of the *ex cathedra* business, however, was to make clear that only one man, and he but rarely, under stringent conditions, speaks for the whole Church.)

The lay Catholic's largest concern is not with the clergy; it is with defining himself in and against the over-all American intellectual milieu. This milieu is pretty much a middle-class affair. What Ortega y Gasset called a "small town philosophy," positivism, more or less, sets the intellectual tone. Among us, there is a general willingness to let ultimate questions go, to concentrate on the proximate ones we can lay hands upon. American intellectual life, in short, is largely aimed at the solution of problems, not at wonder about mysteries; at control over the environment, through social or technological action, not at enjoyment or peace or prayer or leisure or self-discovery. Such intellectual life may be highly successful in turning out a powerful social machine; it grates to shreds the human spirit where faith would take root.

The first task before the Catholic layman on leaving the ghetto is to prove himself before the standards of the powers-that-be in the universities and the publishing or

artistic world. Here the convinced materialists and pragmatists are not ideologically aggressive; they are large-minded
and humane, and their tolerance toward the religious man
is sometimes so thick you can cut it with a knife. The
Catholic intellectual is naturally tempted to disidentify
with his Catholicism, or to mute it into a personal affair
for the religious hours of the week. He is likely to be more
liberal than the liberals or, in a different manner, more
conservative than the conservatives. Since the anti-Semi-
tism of the intellectuals is anti-Catholicism, the temptation
for the Catholic—conservative or liberal—is to be not so
vocally Catholic. And besides, it is a full-time job to keep
up in the academic race for mastery of the pragmatic and
controllable issues.

So the specter of secularized Catholics which the cautious bishop sees lurking in the secular world is not unreal.
The condescending nonbeliever has been all too willing to
help the layman "free himself from the control of the Irish
clergy" (as it would be said if it could be). "Nice going,"
the encouragement may seem to say; "keep evolving; you're
almost free; glad to see you breaking loose; you're almost
one of us." The unbeliever is tempted to think that his own
life is the epitome of Western history: the breaking loose
from the shackles of the Church. All his favorite shibboleths
(one need not deny what truth is in them, only the accompanying myths) suggest his inevitable view of Catholicism:
"the Dark Ages," "the Inquisition," "Enlightenment,"
"Liberty of Conscience."

Caught between the ghetto Catholics who look on his critical and creative efforts as selling out to the Paul Blanshards, and the professional anti-Catholics and large-minded liberals who pat him on the back for his every criticism of the clergy, the Catholic layman soon finds he has to set his mind to the task and forget who is reading him and why. He wants to beware of the emotional rebellion of the adolescent; he wants to beware of the Olympian view that reconciles everything and changes nothing. One of his great loves, for many the greatest, is the Church, and he cares about her critically. The clergy is always in danger of complacency, blindness, or abuse of its responsibilities; the laity is prone to its own occupational hazards; the nonbeliever is prone to succumbing to the spirit of his age. There is a great deal for the lay Catholic qua Catholic to be critical about.

When the Church is grown up, there is a kind of tacit balance of power between those who, laymen and clerics, make up the Church. As Newman said, the clergy may be the head of the Mystical Body, but they'd look quite ridiculous without any laymen. And while the power of the clergy is the moral suasion of command, censure, and excommunication, that of the laity is public opinion, the pen, the voice. The role of the educated layman is not to traipse along behind, yea-saying, but to be out in front taking the risks, beginning the assimilation of new cultures and new discoveries.

On the school question of 1962, for example, it is doubt-

ful that laymen—if consulted—would have acted in the
way the outspoken clerical leaders acted. (It is even doubt-
ful, from signs in the wind, that all the bishops—if consulted—would have supported the outspoken ones. By a
venerable tradition, one bishop does not publicly contradict
another, and thus the first one to speak seizes a significant
tactical advantage.) Lay opinion is clearly divided on the
role and importance of the parochial schools, and on the
reasonableness of bills before the Congress. The danger of
the public school's becoming arms of an *État enseignant*—
perhaps in the hands of loyal Americans of the John Birch
variety—and of their tacit inculcation of positivism, is ugly
to contemplate. *The Commonweal* has argued that the
right to maintain a dissenting school system should not be
financially penalized, but has urged that Catholics consider
the present common good of the nation before their own
needs; and this position, it seems to me, represents the
complexity of the situation.

In other perennial domestic conflicts, like civil birth-
control laws and censorship, it is important to see that
the Latin way of dealing with a moral question is, often
enough, to slap down a general law or prohibition and to
make the individual seek freedom by exception. Anglo-
Saxon minds try to give the benefit to liberty, and to close
off abuses case by case. These two different *styles* often
clash even where there is substantive agreement. Harvard
professors watch over the reading matter and movie-going
of their children; but Catholic Boston bans by public law.

What then will be the effects of the Vatican Council on America? The work of the clergy is primarily to consolidate, to conserve, to speak officially and clearly. In an important sense, the hierarchy works *behind* the present, in the past, upon issues ripe and mature. Issues that are ambiguous wait for another generation or two. Even the great achievements of Pope John XXIII rested on a wide base of eighty years' research and critical discussion.

The Church is not much impressed by the "spirit of the age"—any age. But the layman has in our age the ideas of human equality, dignity, freedom, progress to meditate upon—ideas closely related to the Judeo-Christian vision of man, but realizable today more concretely than heretofore. More than the cleric, he comes into contact with these ideas in their social and political context. In these matters, he is the leader, the cleric follows behind. Let us explore this relationship.

3 The Priest

Part of the difficulty in establishing the role of the priest in America is due to historical changes in society: the separation of Church and State, pluralism, popular education, and the like. Part is also due to the spiritual inheritance of American Catholicism. What happens to the priest in America is important for the world because it is in America that the new forms of civilization are being nurtured and that a new Christian humanism is taking root, as both Christopher Dawson and Jacques Maritain have noticed.

But many things in our land conspire to confuse the role of the priest. The presidential campaign of 1960 showed that in many areas of our country the words "ecclesiastical pressures" conjured up an ominous and ugly image and that "priesthood" is still a word of superstition. On the other hand, the Hollywood image, as in *Going My Way*, seems intent on proving that the priest is a "regular guy;" even in *Pollyanna* the fearsome minister had to be converted and become a friend of all. It is as though the psyche of America, deeply scarred by its experiences with theocratic Protestantism in its early history and with the more or less autocratic clerical types which it knew in Europe, is engaged in a struggle to assimilate a difficult figure in its world view. Early propaganda explicitly described America as a new world and as a paradise; and perhaps implicitly as an escape from the sinful and tangled past of Europe. It was as though America would be the land without original sin, the land of a new humanism built by reason in the high flood of the Enlightenment.

In this view, expressed in the writings of Thomas Paine and the good but secular life of Benjamin Franklin, and preserved in many of our academic environments today, a role for the priest is difficult to find. He is a relic of the past, a past that is not admired. The modern Protestant, proud of the influence his congregationalist and individualist theory have had upon the formation of American democracy, has more and more democratized his own clergy. The transition in *Pollyanna* from fire-and-brimstone to friendliness seems to symbolize quite well the spiritual and social evolution of the Protestant clergy. But in Italy too the American priest and seminarian is probably distinguishable from his European counterparts by a humanness and humor of view that is quite refreshing. As Father Ong has pointed out, the American pastor is also a building pastor, who knows the language of builders and fund raisers; he has thus kept himself in the everyday world of men. His European counterpart is often far more aloof, even austere. It is even likely that younger American priests inherit the congenial, friendly attitudes more markedly than their elders who are closer to Europe.

But at what point can the young priest draw the line in being a regular guy? Where does his identification with the laity begin and where does it end? The modern emphasis upon the apostolate of the laity has also, like the factors mentioned above, helped confuse the role of the priest. Externally, the expectations of people around him, within the flock and without, have changed. Internally, his own spiritual development is pulled in this way and that: to silence and to action, to human development and denial, to affability and restraint. It is difficult for the priest to find himself.

In nearly every culture but our own, the social significance of the priesthood was not only great but central. Whether by special talent of mind or imagination, or physical appearance, or early consecration, a priest was chosen to stand apart from and above other men. His counsels were important if not crucial; often he was the highest leader; if not, his knowledge about the past, opinions about the future, and symbolic power over the unknown forces of life were essential to the man who was. The early priest seemed to have combined in his person the roles of priest, prophet, and king; in fact, it was into this pattern of symbolism that Christ Himself was born, though the three functions had by that time been separated in practice. The splitting of these functions began early, but the social symbolism remained intact; in the days of Greece and Rome the power of the priest and the magistrate was singleminded. Only in early Christian culture did ecclesiastical affairs begin to be stoutly defended as independent of secular affairs, and the historical process of distinction begin. In the Nestorian councils, the Church fought bitterly for the right to determine her own doctrine and her own line of bishops, independently of questions of empire and political peace. In later times, emperors and kings grew restive under clerical power, and the people grew restive under the kings. A thousand years of political evolution have given us democracies and republics in which the role of the priest has changed often and nearly always in a fashion which has delimited his functions more and more narrowly.

Still, even today, the stature of a priest as "another Christ" and as a man of education and authority is carried over to some extent into social and civic matters. Thus the priest of today has behind him a long history in which he has possessed at least a twofold status. He has represented not only the spiritual authority of Christ (which extends to some temporal-spiritual or "mixed" matters like marriage) but also the social authority of secular prestige and influence. Modern times, however, have marked a decline in this second status, for widespread higher education and the maturing of the modern fields of specialization have produced many other leaders than the priest: lawyers, doctors, business and labor leaders, intellectuals and artists, the ministers of many religions, and even many from among the ordinary public. The priest, then, can no longer take for granted his place of prestige in secular society; he is one among many and will have little more influence than his energy and talents earn. Given the tradition of anti-clerical-ism, which lives on in its own forms even in America, he will have even less.

Moreover, the leadership in education which the priest once held has gradually been lost since the Enlightenment. Modern education no longer follows the curricula of the medieval universities; most men seem to feel that our civi-lization, with whatever loss, owes many of its advances, political and humane as well as material, to the shift. At any rate, the priest is no longer among the few who are edu-cated; he is among the many; and the mainstream of edu-cation does not parallel his own but diverges from it. His education is now seen as specialized, with its own jargon and viewpoints. It is no longer a classical education, "uni-versal" or "liberal" in Cardinal Newman's sense; rare is the seminary in which the classes in Greek and in Latin are not simply a gesture toward a dying or dead tradition and in which classes in modern literature, history, and social studies have taken up the slack. The seminary is isolated; it is not ordinarily in a university milieu. The professors in the nonecclesiastical subjects are not ordinarily specialists, pro-ducing and creative in their fields; sometimes they are teach-ing merely because assigned to teach. The seminary library is ordinarily thin in literature, sociology, politics, psychol-ogy, economics; the periodicals are mainly religious, Catho-lic, and popular. In the isolation of the seminary, the professors of philosophy and theology rarely have an oppor-tunity to take an active contemporary part in modern political, literary, scientific, and even religious discussions. Their fields no longer represent leadership in modern intellectual circles; and even within their fields, Catholic work is, not without some justice, in poor repute. There are exceptions to these strictures, of course; but I believe it will be found that they are exceptions in great part because they fulfill the criteria mentioned and have grown strong in swimming against the stream. The faculties of many seminaries are small, ingrown, overworked, and not contemporary in their outlook. A seminary student once said a professor of his had "one of the best minds of the fifteenth century;" and the humor of the jab lay in the ingenuity of expressing the professor's competence together with his liability.

Another change in modern civilization is that art no longer looks to the Church for patronage; young artists, in fact, are often among the most anti-clerical, while priests are among the least appreciative of the arts, classical and especially modern. Of course, ordinary people in general have lost touch with the arts, and it is not to be expected that the priest rise always above his origins. Many of the difficulties in the matter of censorship arise from this alienation of artist from people, and artist from priest; where there is little sympathy, understanding is blocked. In politics, too, the priest plays a lesser part than he was wont to do; when he does try to use influence by swaying others, even through nonviolent picketing or letter-writing, it is resented. Perhaps resentment springs from memories of the past, perhaps in part from the ambiguities of role still inherent in the situation. At any rate, in most lands the priest plays no greater part in politics than other professional men or other men in general, exception made perhaps for the influence and kind of his opposition to communism. Just as men today are more educated than before, so the social arrangement is more sensitive. Powers are better defined, and organized pressures are more quickly felt and more deeply resented.

Even on religious and theological subjects, the ordinary people hear many speakers, gain many ideas and insights, see many varied forms of worship, apart from what they learn from their own priest. The result is that in our pluralistic civilization, the people are free in the priest's presence in a way never experienced before. When they submit to him in doctrinal and moral matters, it is not because they are overawed by his social stature or greater learning or because they have nothing else against which to compare what he tells them. It is because they make an act of faith that his authority comes from Christ. It is because they possess the simplicity of free and willing obedience, precisely one of the notes most proper to the Gospels. The attitude of the laity toward the priest can perhaps be more definite and single-minded now than before. Western culture is perhaps losing the layers of nonessential clerical authority.

It is true that in some lands the transition to this new freedom has at first been tragic. New freedom tends to be intoxicating; the old confusion of spiritual and social status is slow to clarify. For a whole generation or more, the transition can wreak disastrous gaps in the practice of the love that should be shown to God and neighbor. On the other hand, for those persons and those lands who do mature to such obedience in faith, the obedience of free men standing erect as Charles Péguy used to say, there is a great gain in clarity of motive and relationship. The priest does not rule the flock as a tyrant does his subject peoples, or even as a paterfamilias used to rule his slaves, but as a father does his grown and free sons—"not as the rulers of the gentiles. . . ." And perhaps it is true that the good father puts himself in second place.

The peasant classes of Europe were wont to invest the priest with much more authority than this, perhaps a little as the rulers of the gentiles. In Italy it is still the custom to kiss the priest's hand, while kneeling before him, as it was once the custom to greet a liege lord; the respect of the Irish for the priest and, perhaps similarly, of the people of the Tyrol for their priests (the cultural leaders in the enduring attempt to maintain independence from England and Italy) is quite well known. But the descendants of these peasants, in America now, may well be beginning to deny to the priest some of the attributes, like quasi-infallibility, they once implicitly seemed to grant him. They may reason that if the popes have recently had to call for liturgical reform, for a revival of Thomism, and for several other new currents of activity, then things have not been all they should. When they see priests disagreeing among themselves, they begin to understand the freedom that is allowed to prudential judgment of concrete situations, on which differences are bound to thrive.

Thus, due to the social changes of the last centuries, not yet at their culmination in the civilization that is to take shape from our own, the role of the priest in a pluralistic land is trying. A vast range of excellences is required of him. His every fault grates on sophisticated, and specialized, nerves. The freedom of the layman is a heady freedom; habits of anti-clericalism persist, especially where they are stimulated by habits of clericalism that have not yet disappeared. In a transition period genial equilibrium is hard to maintain. Only the simplicity of freely yielded intelligence, in faith, gives the priest effective authority, and even then not in his own name, but in Christ's. And yet this yielding is at the heart of Christianity, a splendid ever-renewed miracle. Priest and people take up mature relationship, as fallible human beings, at this point.

If the priest's relations with others were the only difficulty with the pressure of modern change, his lot would be easier than it is. His most painful task is in the orientation of his own inner life. It is often, though, it must be stressed, not always, observable that the spiritual formation given in the seminary has its roots in cultures far different from our own, ones whose obstacles to Christian life and advantages for Christian life were different from our own. In such cases much of seminary spiritual formation is irrelevant and could not in fact be continued except in the hothouse isolation of the seminary; in priestly practice it wilts away.

Where the public prayers, rules, and mental attitudes inculcated in the seminary derive from the European piety of the last few centuries, they are not simple, in touch with contemporary reality, or directly reminiscent of the Gospels. To the American of our day, they seem overlaid with uncongenial sentiment, a strange legalistic attitude toward God, and narrow suspicion. Not a few books on the seminary rule and on growth in spiritual perfection seem to delight in driving the soul to more and more precise observance; there is in them little sense of enlargement, wholesomeness, freedom, and love, such as one gets in reading the Gospels. They lead away from the experience of God to the observance of discipline; yet they are not so demanding and deep-searching as the works of St. John of the Cross and St. Teresa, which are not read with near the frequency or attention. It might even be said that, by their dwelling on the observance of discipline, they conduce to a comfortable mediocrity and the easy appearance of platitudes on the lips.

The young priest has to make up his own mind on each of these questions, but the difficulty is that the more intent on spiritual growth he is, the more he may have given himself to uncritical docility. His spirituality, therefore, may end up being a borrowed light, never seized by his own independent judgment and rooted permanently and personally in his own intellect and will. The danger is great that the Jansenist strain so deeply rooted in most of the national stocks from which our priests spring will be passed on uncritically from generation to generation and that some young American clerics will strain every nerve during their seminary days to convince themselves of last century European attitudes which they do not share. It is a shame when afterward, as priests, they scuttle much of what they spent years trying to learn because it is unrealistic. Then comes the temptation to throw out everything that they learned.

The task of the priest to grow up into the stature of a full human being of the late twentieth century and to grow up into the stature of Christ, is terribly difficult, because, for the most part, it must be done without guides. The riches of spirituality in the American spirit have hardly been noticed, let alone tapped; often the typically American virtues are stifled or at least warned against, perhaps because of the misunderstandings about "Americanism" a half-century ago. The young American priest, when he is faithful to his own best insights and spirit, is a new kind of priest and is working out a new image of spirituality. Perhaps some day one of them will set the new way down in writing, and the many will not feel so much alone.

As the external social events of the centuries have served to strip down the role of the priest to its priestly, Christlike essentials, so perhaps the new kind of holiness will be only "the more excellent way" of which St. Paul speaks, less legalistic, more fully human because divine, redolent of freedom and love. To maintain such holiness in the complexities of our age will be witness indeed to Christ. It will reach to the heart of our civilization, as did the witness of Pope John.

4 A Christian Empiricism

The bishop or the religious superior whose preoccupying concern is a building program and tightened moral observance, thinks that he is realistic. Before him he sees the "facts" of building needs, the hard realities of raising money, the obvious brick-and-glass assets, the sense of well-heeled subordinates who heed unquestioningly his or "tradition's" moral discipline. On the other hand, another kind of bishop or religious superior or layman, whose preoccupying concern is "souls," "witness," "intellectual life" or "emerging laymen," thinks that he is realistic. Less concerned about pragmatic, administrative or legal spirit, less observant of convention, very critical at least implicitly of the Church's poor showing in the last few centuries and of her rather uninspiring aspects in present-day America, these men like to think of themselves, not as idealists, but as the real realists. The first group calls the second "idealists," "dreamers," or—worse yet—"liberals." The second group calls the first "activists," "clericals," "legalists," or "conservatives."

Just what is a Christian realism for America?

It is important to talk about a Christian realism, or empiricism, *for America,* because one-half the difficulties of our adolescent nation, within and without the Church, lie in her failure to grasp her own identity, her differences from other nations, her dependences and independences. America has not yet rationally taken hold of herself. Insecure, she sometimes scorns where she might better honor; is subservient where she might better stand up and lead. The American Church is equally as insecure, as alternately scornful of, and too subservient to, other members of the Church Universal.

But it is more important to talk first about a Christian realism in general. And perhaps it is time. For years, discussion has prepared the ground for the definition of a Christian philosophy. The problem of a Christian empiricism is the same problem. What is the relation of faith and nature? Generalities about grace building on nature are guiding lines, not nearly adequate enough. A great deal has happened to man's knowledge of nature and natural society; and faith too, pruned and tried by centuries of conflict, has been maturing. The discoveries of depth-psychology, for example, are stimulating a new penetration of the theology of grace, and are gradually converting discussion into psychological terms. Theologies of human history are being written. Pluralist Christian societies are exerting claims to status as equal to or superior to sacral Christian societies. Catholic universities threaten to come apart at the seams in their straining for a synthesis that will hold the manifold secular sciences in a Christian vision (however true it may be that too many universities still prefer to hide from the problem, and do not ask the searching questions).

For faith and Christianity have been maturing in silence, and almost in retreat. As the world turned over, stretched, threw off the blankets of the Middle Ages, and grew from childhood to manhood very swiftly—as the sciences advanced incredibly, as political maturity emerged, along with literacy and sophistication, and modern economics, and medicine, and critical philosophy—the faith has been quiet and in the background. Before, the favorite image for the Church was the mother caring for her child. It is perhaps time to use also, along with the first, the image of the maiden preparing herself for marriage: so has the Church these recent centuries awaited the growth of Western Culture to manhood.

The problem of a Christian empiricism seems, then, to bring about a marriage between the Church and culture. No longer can grown men be treated as children, or secular culture as a child. The educated layman sometimes knows as much of moral theology, and even of doctrine, as does the priest. Society as a whole is more and more used to being wooed, not bullied, appealed to as free and mature, not arbitrarily commanded. Nor is this change in expectation due only to a loss of the sense of authority. A father treats his sons differently than he treats servants, and authority does not suffer. A husband moves his wife with love, and authority does not suffer. It is not the mode of commanding that is essential for obedience, but the union of wills. Free men obey beautifully when they stand erect; God calls men friends, no longer servants; love is perfect only where judgment is informed, free, and mature. Authorities who block information, freedom, or maturity of judgment do not move men as God does, and quite fail to be perfect as He is. They mock, rather than imitate, His authority. But let us stay on this point a moment, for it brings other data into focus.

Authority will always have to command the unpleasant, the seemingly irrational, the humanly impractical—the cross—but it need not think such commands the essence of obedience. Rather they are the fruit of sin and human blindness. Men do not know the future; views diverge. Thus, for action's sake, there must be both rulers and ruled. But sin and passion have hurled still more confusion into the hurtling warp and woof of events. How many good things tangle and are destroyed for earthly use! The superior who commands does well to recognize that he, as well as his free subjects, must bear the weight of the added unintelligibility sin sows through history; so many things cannot make sense on earth. The cross is the one triumph over this pain, irrationality, impracticality: triumph not by fleeing it, or changing it, but by submitting to it with patience. The world never likes to learn about the cross, for it seems to remember a halcyon time when there was no call for it. But the Church must woo all she can to learn of it: to be realistic, to triumph. Every aspect of our maturing society must be approached and courted, that there be "filled up the sufferings of Christ."

Thus the data for considering the problem of Christian empiricism are manifold. There is Church and hierarchy; there is a maturing and widely sophisticated society; there is the nature of obedience and freedom; there is sin, the cross, and triumph; there is world-courting impetus of Christian love. The approaches to this data are most often only twofold. The conservatism we spoke of in the first paragraph stresses the obedience of servants to king. The liberalism we spoke of stresses the freedom of responsible men. Both positions hark back to political images of monarchy or democracy. Both get tangled up in various other sociohistorical movements that admit of "conservative" or "liberal" opposition. Neither position goes far enough in interpreting the data. Nor is a "liberal conservatism" or "conservative liberalism" anything but a patch-and-glue solution. One must tie the liberal-conservative debate to its epistemological roots.

Just as a Christian realism is a habitual attitude of mind that is adequate to reality, so other "isms," liberal or conservative, are attitudes of mind that are less adequate to reality. The essential point is that the roots of our discussion concern the adequacy of various attitudes of mind. More, these attitudes of mind are usually unconscious, unscrutinized, too deep and basic in each man to be often questioned; they are assumed, and all other questions spring from them. The solution of the problem of Christian empiricism then (and of a Christian philosophy) lies in making conscious, taking in hand, and rectifying our habitual attitude toward reality. In short, it is an epistemological problem; for reality comes to us only according to the purity of our reception.

There can be, it seems, only three fundamental positions toward reality. It is difficult even to conceive others, for every attempt seems to involve the other three. A man can busy himself in data; he can hypothesize about data; he can verify and affirm his hypotheses. In all its rovings from horizon to horizon of the universe, the human mind plays on these three fundamental acts. Theologians act no differently. Businessmen study trends, project long-term hypotheses, verify them against past experience or other factors. A ball player sizes up the game, the pattern and force of the opposition, likely openings, and draws upon past skill and experience before lunging ahead with his strategy. The scientist collects facts, turns then to mathematical schemes, comes back and verifies. The housewife's "intuition" worked in the past. Thus every man can be realistic in his own domain. True, the field of some men's experience of facts is larger; the capacity of some men's ideas is greater; and the sureness of some men's judgments is better trained. But in all fields experience, meaning, and judgment are what men live by.

Now some men have stronger tendencies toward one of these levels than toward another; and many who possess ability on all three levels suffer from not explicitly grasping the fact that there are three levels. Hence these sometimes join forces inauspiciously with those who are operating on only one level—inauspiciously, for to operate on only one of these levels is to operate off-balance. And to lock arms with those off-balance may end in righting the errant, but more probably in rocking oneself.

Finally, I would suggest that what is generally called "the conservative" is usually the man who operates on the level of experience; and what is called "the liberal" is usually the man who operates on the level of meaning. The advantage of this way of distinguishing "conservative" from "liberal" is considerable. The builder of buildings, the invoker of tradition—see if he does not prefer facts to meaning. Look at the patron of dynamic Christianity, or progress and new ideas—see if he does not prefer meaning to facts. See, too, how one gets on the other's nerves: each thinks important exactly what the other likes to brush off as secondary, what will "take care of itself." What is important to the one are the phenomena that can now be seen in motion; what is important to the other is the meaning latent in the phenomena that cries for ever greater manifestation—and hence perhaps for break-up of much of the existing phenomena.

As long as experience is pitted against meaning, conservative against liberal, object against subject, facts against ideas, pragmatism against thought, expedience against utopianism, there is no way out of countless dilemmas. To pit one against the other is already to have posed the problem poorly. Hence it is already an epistemological error. To unite them side-by-side is equally wrong, for experience is not idea, nor idea experience; they are on different levels.

The theologian, the businessman, the ball player, the

housewife, the scientist, go first to data, then to meaning, then to verification and judgment. When we are at our best, the first thing we want are the facts. Then we seek meaning. ("Oh! I get it!") Then we move towards affirming the meaning as adequate to the situation. ("Wait a minute! Sounds good! But is it true?") After laying the meaning to the facts, and assuring ourselves we're in a position to read the measurement fairly (for even a ruler tells lies if looked at from an angle), we can safely claim to know what we're saying. In short, the movement of human knowing is from experience of data, to positing of meaning, to a virtually all-scrutinizing judgment.

It is important to notice that once a man starts this movement (of itself it is restless until it passes all three levels), he can stop it anywhere. He can choose his level; knowledge is laborious. Still, having new experiences, we are not yet content. Going on toward ordering them and conjecturing new hypotheses, we are still not satisfied. Only in affirmation, when reached at the full extent of our power and of the available evidence, do we find some rest. Being finite, it is the best we can do. (And even to the most humanly certain of things we can ask "Why?" and expect that some day men will know more than we do now.) New experiences constantly upset parts of old affirmations. A steady, marching base—a core—always stays the same. But the new experiences set us to marching methodically (if we are wise) toward ever wider vision and grasp, an ever-increasing core of corporate knowledge, with an ever wider projection of anticipations into the future.

In this way, experience is not opposed to meaning; it stimulates search for it. Meaning is not opposed to experience; it grows out of it. But neither experience nor meaning is yet reality. Not until the mind verifies both experience and meaning has a man grasped reality. *Christian empiricism exists only on this third level of human knowing, that of verified affirmation.* Christian empiricism is not experience alone, for experience is only a beginner's level. Christian empiricism is not ideas alone, for ideas can be of centaurs, phlogiston, and anything at all, not always verifiable in experienced data. Christian empiricism is meaning grasped in data and affirmed as grasped. Christian empiricism is wed to facts (all facts of nature and of revelation), but it is not positivism for positivism lacks meaning. Christian empiricism loves ideas, but it is not idealistic because idealism cares nothing for verification. Christian empiricism is beyond both positivism and idealism, in the same way as human judgment is beyond phenomena and conceptions, or in the same way as the real meaningful world is beyond mere facts or mere ideas. Christian empiricism is intensely personal, for judgment cannot live in books (though facts and ideas can) but only in persons; and the real world, its object, echoes too far into the infinite to be caught, quite, on paper, or even in discourse.

Again, it will be seen that Christian empiricism depends first on wisdom and, secondly, on as much freedom of discussion as possible. For wisdom alone—before science or understanding even begin—can insure that *all* relevant facts be faced, and it is with facts that the dynamism begins.

And free discussion is human society's best approximation to infinite wisdom. Thus the suitability of democracy's love of free, mature self-criticism can hardly be overestimated in our striving for a Christian empiricism; while the adherence of a Christian empiricism to a living core of divine tradition and critical certitude gives democracy's freedom a systematic and dynamic unity. Thus, even the monks of old used to love to ask the youngest among them to express his opinion on matters of the common good, thinking that wisdom speaks even in the humblest. For the monks, as for any society, the superior's decision (and it is his alone), once all the facts are in, is final. The human approach to wisdom, free discussion, is no hindrance to obedience; neither is it essential. It is, however, the most admirable, most natural, approach.

There can be no automatic production of Christian realists. Only those can affirm who grasp their own power to affirm, grasp its extent and limits, and hence affirm consciously and clearly according to the degree of verification they attain. Man easily fools himself. Error is easy. Wisdom is not so common as foolishness. No easy rules, only the hard work of never being satisfied as long as questions remain unanswered, leads to judgments finally adequate to reality. The mind is in some sense all things, but it never reaches that term existentially until the final Vision, and hence must always be asking, searching, confirming. Christian realism has no rest on earth.

There is, then, the problem of a Christian realism *for*

America. Although a subject for which adequate distinctions are not yet forged, it deserves insistent attention. I suggest that the great crisis in American Catholic life is to distinguish itself from its European heritage. Further, this distinction will entail outgrowing two opposed positions—and in fact it is the inheritance of this opposition that is our most needless trial. On the one hand, ecclesiastical formation of the American clergy is still reductively European, either because many of the young men study abroad, or because the French-Sulpician and Latin-textbook influence on our seminaries is still—since the environment is sheltered—far stronger than the same influence can possibly be on the realities of American Catholic life. This ecclesiastical formation, furthermore, is greatly characterized by that conservative attention to facts or to experience of which we have spoken at some length (though, in this case, the facts or experience are largely of *systems* of moral and dogmatic theology, whose examples and conceptual backgrounds are taken from nontechnological, nondemocratic social life).

On the other hand, most of the ideas of the modern Catholic revival have also been generated in Europe, chiefly in France. And the spirit of *hypothèse*, the readiness to explore a new idea which we spoke of as the second level of human knowing, is more natural to the French than to Americans. Thus the opposed spirits of an old-time European conservatism and the modern French-led revival (a Catholic conservatism and a Catholic liberalism) both come to thrive on the American scene, though neither have a great deal in common with that "practical creativity" that seems America's most original talent. Eminently creative and ready to change, America's genius is not conservative; and eminently close to facts and verification, Anglo-Saxon rather than Rousseauistic in its common-man approach, it is not liberal in the Continental sense. The sooner America, and American Catholicism, grasps its own identity in this respect, many of the frictions now felt will dissolve, and the more real ones belonging to its life's work will emerge.

Thus it seems one must agree with Maritain's verdict in *Reflections on America* that America is nearer to the concrete historical ideal of his "true humanism" than any other nation in history. Americans are closer in spirit to a Christian realism than Europe ever was or perhaps can be. For Americans love facts; but they are young and curious for meaning too. Neither traditionalists nor prophets, living still in a kind of innocence, they wish to be, above all, wise and good and loved. This gives them boundless practical optimism and creativity. Committed to twentieth century civilization more than any one, and strong in faith (and in increasingly learned faith), they are the Western World's second chance at developing a Christian philosophy, a world of earthly culture where faith for the sake of eternity (there is no paradise on earth) weds, and does not dominate save in being loved, man and the things of man.

5 THE NEW ORDER OF THE WORLD

Scenting the promise of America's destiny, Orestes Brownson, Archbishop Ireland, Isaac Hecker and other nineteenth-century Catholics were filled with joy in that first spring of the American Church. They foresaw a new kind of Catholicism, for a new type of man: the free man who was being fashioned as an example to the world. America was to be *Novus Ordo Seclorum: The New Order of the World* (so reads the dollar bill), built beneath the eye of justice. The intervening generations of Americans let much of that promise, that justice, slip from their grasp. Complacent, self-righteous, superior, they mouthed ancient words on Independence Day. They did little to combat nativist, religious, racist injustice in their midst. The good, kind simple folk were also deep in small prejudices, fears, and thick self-righteousness. The rebellious artists, writers, and professors came to scorn their kind-hearted blindness. In those years, the American people and their cultural leaders, their defenders, were split apart; to the present, the split has not been healed. Without roots, the intellectuals lost their hard grip on the realities of the land in which they lived, on the chief of the realities: the people. They chased the dream of a foreign experiment. The ordinary people ceased to dream. Suddenly, for both, there was nothing left.

Bombs fell, terror shrieked in the night, political betrayals of whole nations happened yearly, a hundred million persons died by violence. Moreover, afterward, on awakening from the Second World War and Korea and Hungary, Americans found that what they had been seeing was no nightmare. It was reality, to be lived with day by day. "What has happened to the American dream?" William Faulkner wrote of that apathy. "We dozed, slept, and it abandoned us. There no longer sounds a unifying voice speaking our mutual hope and will." The year 1960 was a watershed year. It marked the last year of Eisenhower, the end of an era. Eisenhower was small-town America. At the white gate of his Gettysburg farm, he stood for the values and the myths and the complacency of the average American: he was "such a good man." He was the good fruit of the generations through which he had lived. But in his last year of office, he and other leading Americans began to realize that America had lost its identity. The complacency and the clichés no longer hid the loss.

Ten of the most serious and respected Americans (no Catholic among them) agreed to contribute to a symposium on "The National Purpose." So grave was the public sense of need that the staid New York Times published the symposium concurrently with an organ of the mass media, the picture magazine Life.[1] When in history has a nation so felt itself unsure of its purposes, while yet in its

[1] The National Purpose. Life Magazine series. Holt, Rinehart and Winston, 1960.

youth and at the flood-tide of its resources? The moment was full of drama. Mr. Kennedy, then Senator from Massachusetts and nominee as presidential candidate of his party, awakened old traditions and new hope with his slogan of a "New Frontier." He spoke harshly, pessimistically, of the situation of America. The truth from all these sources, penetrating through generations of illusion, seemed to revive her. The bitter winds of the cold war had shaken loose old branches; a second spring was being offered America. Or so it seemed.

The separation of intellectuals and people had brought America nearly to destruction. A nation cannot live without the truth, and if her dreamers and her thinkers abandon her people to cheap and vulgar hucksters, not even the old-fashioned integrity of an Eisenhower can save her. A nation needs leaders who love their people and speak the truth. It needs leaders who are not afraid of the hard, empirical, political work of effective social action, who are not afraid of risk, violence, or even the shedding of blood in opposing the passions of prejudice and inequality. But leaders arise from the people. Parents in each home, teachers in each school, businessmen and professional men in each office, men in each union, must favor leaders who speak the truth, no matter how ugly and how harsh. In a democracy, each man counts; each man's illusion corrupts the circle in which he lives.

Moreover, in the second spring of America, Catholics will play a larger role than in the first. Catholics are over forty-million strong, one in every four Americans. If they learn to love the truth, to open their eyes and see the needs of their neighbors and their land, if they live the Gospels, then a great moral force will be unleashed in American life, a sorely needed force. For America has not yet recovered her identity. The breach between people and cultural leaders has not yet been healed. The philosophers and poets of the human spirit are not yet heard through the land. Extremist right-wing voices flounder in the darkness of their own frustration, signal the breakdown of the normal channels of patriotic feeling. Beneath the sound of trucks on our roads, under the rhythms of our daily life, one can hear in the wind the people's questioning: "Whither, America? Where is it you go? Where do you run?"

For this reason, the new generation will long recall that debate of 1960, and reflect on the later course of American life. Three famous statements dramatized the tone, the first that by William Faulkner quoted above. The second was that of Walter Lippman:

The public mood of the country is defensive, to hold on and to conserve, not to push forward and to create. We talk about ourselves as if we were a completed society, one which has achieved its purpose, and has no further great business to transact.

George F. Kennan pointed the question more sharply and more emphatically. He went to the heart of the fear felt by millions of Americans: that after three generations of bravado, we might be only second-best.

If you ask me whether a country—with no highly developed sense of national purpose, with the overwhelming accent of life on personal comfort, with a dearth of public services and a surfeit of privately sold gadgetry, with insufficient social discipline even to keep its major industries functioning without grievous interruption—if you ask me whether such a country has over the long run good chances of competing with a purposeful, serious and disciplined society such as that of the Soviet Union, I must say that the answer is No.

John K. Jessups, an editor of *Life*, opened the debate by noting that America's invocation of a higher law than constitutions and agreements—a law which affirms that "all men are created equal"—had launched a global revolution, not merely a national one. Jessups also issued an Aristotelian call to each citizen to pursue excellence as the foundation of the common good. Adlai Stevenson in his contribution distinguished the private aspect of freedom from the public aspect; in the public aspect of freedom public authority, having the consent of the governed, plays an essential and active part. He urged a return to "the reality principle" and deplored America's concern for the citizen as a private consumer rather than as a mature, responsible American. Archibald MacLeish urged that freedom is open and infinite, ever unachieved and ever beyond present programs— a dream, the American dream. David Sarnoff insisted that the communist plan, protracted in time and space and in a limitless variety of techniques, permits of only two alternatives: surrender or counteroffensive; it is more dangerous to minimize than to maximize the nature of communist intentions.

Billy Graham assailed the cancer of relativism that is sending toxins into the bloodstream of American life and charged that America has the "highest per capita boredom of any spot on earth." John W. Gardner of the Carnegie Foundation addressed himself to the individual citizen; he pleaded for free, responsible commitment and the pursuit of excellence in one's tasks and in one's life: "Every good man strengthens society." Clinton Rossiter argued that Americans, like the children of Israel, are children of destiny and as such have significance for all the nations of the world; America needs, in middle age, to regain her sense of mission: "Having once been great, we cannot endure to be mediocre." Albert Wohlstetter of the RAND Corporation warned that America has many, even conflicting, purposes which demand reasoned and sacrificial choice; oscillation from one purpose to another will not do. He warned that disarmament is desirable but would be costly and more difficult to enforce now than ever before because of the power of even a single nuclear weapon.

James Reston maintained that leadership means innovation; persuasion of the people should follow, not precede, decisions; our great Presidents acted first, then explained. He stressed the moral strength of the "other, quieter America" which is not the America of Hollywood, Madison Avenue, and Washington, and the historic achievements and patience of the American people since World War II. He pleaded for leaders who know how to bring moral ideas and politics together. Walter Lippman closed the debate by urging a definition of means and policies, not of ends, since our end has always been and still is freedom. The task of definition belongs to an innovator of the stature of Theodore Roosevelt, Wilson, and Franklin D. Roosevelt, who as President must re-fashion and re-educate American opinion to the realities and complexities of the contemporary scene.

The really crucial issue in the background of every contribution to the debate was the emergence of a powerful, aggressive rival to the United States: the Russo-Sino bloc. Russia seems to *know* where she is going; her theory and practice are at one in a concerted effort to "bury capitalism." But a society founded on the principles of free discussion and rational choice, like that of the United States, cannot "live by a book" or by an ideology. Thus the ten participants in the debate showed widely different estimates of a variety of sociopolitical facts. In the American view policy must wait upon fact, not upon a manifesto. Even on so crucial an issue as our stance in relation to Russia, the estimates do not seem unanimous: Is Russia an unruly friend? An enemy? A threat to our life? An estimable rival? Should we try to destroy her? Change her? Live with her?

But a whole host of other sociopolitical facts were also disputed. Some of the participants saw America as soft, complacent, and surfeited with private pleasures at the expense of common and grave concerns. Others stressed what they see as the natural and religious strength of the people existing beneath the veneer of advertising and publicity. Some contributors seemed to take at face value the new world-image of Russia as the number-one or soon-to-be number-one world power; others stressed the latent, unused, immeasurable energies of America. Some took for granted a bloc of "free" nations in the world; others cautioned that "free" has many meanings and that sometimes it merely means "not communist." Some argued that in any fair battle of propaganda, ideals of freedom could not fail to be victorious over communism; others noted that common U.S. assumptions about other nations and their preferred course of development have been wrong. But there was one question on which all agreed: America's interests and responsibilities are no longer national, but worldwide.

Alongside the sociopolitical issues raised by the debate, another type of question, which can only be called "philosophical," was awakened, if most often only by implication. These questions entail point of view rather than estimate of fact; no doubt their resolution bears heavily upon subsequent estimate of fact, but in themselves they are distinct and preliminary questions. One of the merits of the debate was that it raised such questions.

The most dramatic of these questions concerns the role of authority in a democracy. Majority opinion is in fact rarely the originator of creative ideas or even of decisions that require sacrifice. A pluralist society has no more than a very general hierarchy of ends by which to guide action. Ascendance to power in a democracy demands assiduous cultivation of an acceptable "public image." At what point, then, can a leader of forcefulness and insight begin to give a nation the determination it has by its own Constitution denied itself from any other source? It seems that belief in democracy depends on belief that a free people can "some-how" generate and recognize its true leaders.

A second philosophical issue is the reliability of a national dream or a national myth as a means of structuring a course of action. Acceptance of a myth seems to demand "a leap," an act of faith that it offers the most realistic and reasonable course. But a myth or a dream is what it is precisely because it has not suffered the critique of wisdom. Hitler gave the Third Reich a myth, but it was neither a good myth nor a reasonable one; the same might be said of the communist paradise and of at least the earlier forms of America's "manifest destiny." Myths about God's favor upon any one nation can lead to disastrous self-righteousness. Modern civilization has almost been destroyed by political messiahs. On the other hand, a middle course between brute realism and utopianism is difficult to reach. Without ideals—which may or may not prove to be viable—and without projections into the future, it seems impossible that reasonable action can take shape.

The point of view from which freedom is to be regarded is also a matter of dispute. Does freedom consist in giving as much as possible to the individual person, and taking the public good and common action as freedom's enemy? In addition to meaning the absence of constraint, does freedom set standards or conditions which must be met, such as commitment, responsibility, and competence? Again, is freedom rooted in blind drives, in ardors of the will, in whim, or in intelligence? Positions on each of these questions lie behind opinions on matters of concrete policy, and arguments on concrete policy usually suffer because these prior positions are not made explicit.

A fourth issue suggested by several essays in the debate is the use of the word "morality." There does not seem to be anywhere an intellectually defensible limit upon human actions, a limit which says, *No, this is wrong.* None of the debaters showed a definite awareness of a universally recognizable dictate of *intelligence* which goes beyond instinct or compulsion, beyond convention, beyond positive law or the voice of authority. Mention was made of a dictate, but one may wonder if it is an intellectually defensible dictate, intelligible through and through; one may also wonder if its absence is not at the root of the Western malaise. Ours is an intellectual society that cannot intellectually defend its own values.

Finally, a fifth philosophical issue concerns the meaning of man, and in a way it summarizes the previous issues. It is not clear from the debate, but some of its participants implied that there is an intellectually defensible reason for preferring the American interpretation of man to the communist. Is one society more suited to man than the other— and verifiably so? If everything is relative, our differences with the Russians are merely differences of sociopolitical power and sociopolitical tension. We are fighting in a jungle, and fighting not for humanity but for America. Though implicitly and vaguely they took a stand concerning this issue, the participants did not enter its depths.

The many issues they raised showed that the participants were well aware of the complexities of the American situation. Moreover, taken in the perspective of the past 300 years, the debate was an important step. At one time the liberal philosophy of the Enlightenment could not have raised such issues. From a doctrinaire point of view, the troubles that America is having simply *should not be*. The irreversible line of progress, the advances of science and technology, the freedom of thought, the might of the economic machine, should have brought us tolerable happiness. But, though we have much sorrow and no millenium, nothing disastrous has occurred; we have simply outgrown a set of doctrines. For 300 years we have in the main avoided philosophic questions and instead turned our attention to political and social reforms and to scientific advancement. Now we find that basic questions regarding what it is to be human must be raised. Our power and techniques outstrip our doctrine; we need guidance for the choices open to us. As Charles Péguy was saying 50 years ago, "The revolution is moral, or not at all." Until now it has been more or less programmatic. We were living off a fund of ideas that we assumed could defend themselves. Now we are faced with the necessity of redefining what we mean by those ideas and of initiating fresh programs to keep them relevant and real. We are faced with what John Henry Newman would call a "Development of Doctrine." We are faced with a crisis inherent in the human condition, the crisis of internal growth.

The recent debate seems to have begun a movement of

intellectual and volitional regeneration. One of the first steps was the debaters' implicit rejection of relativism. The consensus seemed to be that real issues, intellectually defensible issues concerning standards of excellence, are involved in the present struggle. Issues of intellect and will are at stake. The contributors did not generally say so, but the present battle is not one of taste or preference, a purely curious historical struggle between two cultural forces. Surely an implication of the debate is that man measures ideologies, that not everything is relative, and that the present confrontation challenges the whole human race's grasp of its identity and destiny. The participants asked, in a nutshell, what is man?

Second, the debate made an incidental but important step in that it turned to the two historical traditions out of which the modern West has grown: the tradition of the liberal Enlightenment and the tradition of Judeo-Christianity. Not only the contribution of Billy Graham but that of nearly every other participant invoked the language of inner struggle and self-mastery, of messianism, the prophetic spirit, compassion, and moral growth, made part of our culture by the centuries-old Judeo-Christian heritage. The significance of this turn of the discussion is its removal of an anomaly that has long plagued the West, and especially America: the division of the nonreligious men from the religious, the existence of two camps that conceived of themselves as antithetic. For they are in fact the two poles that have always been the source of tension and fecundation of Western life. Unlike other world religions, Judaism and

Christianity are forced by their natures to have a great stake in earthly life and its dilemmas. At the same time it was the religious mind that broke through the pessimism and cyclicism of the Greeks, that conceived of progress in history, that insisted on the reality of the horizons of the spirit. Between these two poles Western civilization has generated a dynamism which is at once of this world and of the spirit, of change and eternity, of process and of law. It claims to be not merely Western, but human. Whatever the situation of individual men within the West, whether as secular humanists or as men of religious faith, the cultural force that makes the present has roots in both traditions, and the exploration in both begun by the recent discussion gives hope of deep and abundant rejuvenation.

The philosophical prong of the on-going debate aims ever more deeply for the recovery of the sources of our inner life. The sociopolitical prong aims at ever more accurate assessment of our changing external life. These two prongs operate together. With both of them at work, we stand a good chance of ranging ourselves on the side of reality and of surviving the contingencies and vicissitudes of time as far as is given us. With either prong dulled or broken, we risk delusion and inevitable perishing. The new generation must educate itself to both these skills, in order to recover the strength of spirit necessary for the new order men desire. Nothing creative comes easily. But the voice of the turtle is already heard in the land, and the earth pushes forth her buds.

6 POPE JOHN'S ENCYCLICALS

The new generation has an incomparable advantage over the generations which preceded it: it has experienced in its youth, as its attitudes and ideals were being formed, the momentous first session of the Second Vatican Council. In that incomparable man, the good Pope John, it has had a taste of what the future of Catholicism can be like; it has no more precious and important task than keeping his spirit alive. Humble, simple, open, free, Pope John was the man in our time who most approximated Aristotle's "man of practical wisdom," the prophets and saints who are touchstones of the spiritual freedom possible to the human person, and the Christ of the Gospels. Pope John is the criterion of Catholic goodness for the men of our generation; each may stand up to him, and be measured. Such measuring will record the degree to which each man becomes himself, is open to others, cherishes freedom and justice. It would betray Pope John to make of *him* a pattern; his very witness was that each man is unique and must serve God according to his own way of perceiving and obeying the general laws of human life.

Pope John had definite ideas about a "new order" of human life. It was to that new order he dedicated his brief life as pope. He desired peace and unity. He insisted that these were founded on truth, freedom, justice, love. He therefore served these foundations, rather than the edifices built on them in the past—built on them only partially. Let us reform and renew the Church at its foundations, was his plea; then perhaps we can speak of peace and unity. He concentrated on the most important things. Those whose chief allegiance is to the secondary things—habits, conventions, practices grown up over hundreds of years— felt threatened. They sometimes fought bitterly. "It will take us fifty years to undo the harm he has wrought," one of them was quoted as saying; and the struggle will indeed go on for years.

But Pope John's Council, and his encyclicals, brought about a change in principle and mood. At the highest position of the Church, down through the majority of the council of bishops, the idea of reform had taken hold. The chief point of reform was that of liberty: liberty to study, liberty to discuss, liberty to differ, liberty to converse with all other men. How could the Church of Christ ever have lost liberty? But it had. The wave of enthusiasm and relief that swept the Church and the world arose because of its return and because of the return of Catholics into the midst of the human race, out of their defensive isolation.

Philosophically speaking, Pope John's two great encyclicals, *Mater et Magistra* and *Pacem in terris*, have two great achievements to their credit. On the one hand, they by-passed Latin Scholasticism and returned for their central inspiration to a more authentic philosophic tradition of the Church. On the other hand, they moved the philosophic attitude of the Church in the same direction as that in which Anglo-American philosophy seems to be moving, making these two philosophies peculiarly relevant to each other. Both of these achievements are of the utmost histori-cal importance.

Less than a century ago, studying in Rome, John Henry Newman was appalled at the state of Latin Scholasticism. Pope Leo XIII was likewise distressed; he called for a serious philosophical reform within the Church, insisting that the sources be studied anew. The great tragedy of the Catholic philosophy of the time was that it did not even understand its own tradition. Memorized definitions and logical manipulations had replaced authentic philosophy; scandalously inept textbooks had replaced both the source books and creative work. The secular philosophic world held in polite contempt what Maritain has called "the seven centuries of Catholic laziness." It is impossible to understand the significance of Pope John's *Mater et Magis-tra* and *Pacem in terris* without adverting to the yeast placed in Catholicism by Leo XIII some eighty years ago. That yeast had been operating all the years that Angelo Giuseppe Roncalli was growing to the fullness of his vocation.

Because of this long ambiguity within the Catholic tradition it has been difficult to describe the conflicting philosophical attitudes at the Second Vatican Council. Those who are called traditionalists or conservatives generally profess allegiance to the Latin Scholastic tradition, particularly as it was expressed after Trent and taught in the Roman universities in the nineteenth and early twentieth centuries. Those who are called reformers, or liberals, or of the open-door school, are generally those whose ultimate allegiance is to the earlier tradition of the Church: to Scripture, to the historical study of the Fathers (Greek as well as Latin), and to the liturgical life of the early Church. Pope John chose for his own view the description "pastoral." That this designation is not meant to be opposed to "theological," "intellectual," or "scientific" may be grasped from the fact that the reforming party at the Council drew its strength precisely from the most prolific writers, scholars, and theoreticians in the present Church. The Council is a scholarly one if ever there was one; all reports stress its formal, educative impact in bringing the bishops into contact with modern scholarship.

But Pope John's program, like the Council's thus far, is different in style from Latin Scholasticism; and the differences are hard to characterize in a single descriptive phrase. Understandably, those accustomed to viewing the world in the manner of Latin Scholastics are outraged at having their viewpoint seriously impugned; it is difficult for them to believe they have been that wrong, or even only half wrong. It is even difficult for them to accept the possibility of another point of view than their own. Are they not *Romani?*

Are they not—yes, even—the Church? But whatever their glories, and in spite of their contrary assumption, the Latin Scholastics cannot claim Aquinas as their mentor; they cannot claim the worldview, only the words, of Aristotle. There is a serious discontinuity between Aquinas and the late Scholastics; Fr. de Broglie's famous article on faith in *Gregorianum* is one witness to the gap.

The emphasis which Aristotle places on the individual person in the *Nichomachean Ethics*, for example, and the emphasis he places on historical development and "what is" rather than "what ought to be" in his *Politics*, are clearly present in Pope John's encyclicals; they are not present in the moral handbooks of the Latin Scholastics. Aristotle, and Aquinas after him, refuse to turn ethics into a logical or legal system, and insist on the element of risk in moral decision; the Latin Scholastics coalesce ethics and canon law, and minimize risk and individuality. Again, Latin Scholasticism finds it meaningful to distinguish "thesis" from "hypothesis" in the question of Church and State; such a distinction might be operative in Plato's *Republic*, but it is meaningless in the methodology of Aristotle's political philosophy.

Aquinas for his part, as Eric D'Arcy's *Conscience and Its Right to Freedom* has recently shown, had all the reasons of the Gospels for insisting more than Aristotle on the equality and dignity of all men, not only of philosophers. The Christian tradition, not the Greek, elaborated the notion of conscience, and Aquinas benefited by that elaboration. The doctrine of human rights is more highly developed in Aquinas than, for example, Reinhold Niebuhr in a recent note in *Christianity and Crisis* on *Pacem in terris* intimates; but it was not quite complete, except in principle, and it is, to modern eyes, inconsistently applied. The political writings of Jacques Maritain on the person and the common good, however, which cohere almost to the letter with Pope John's encyclicals, derive from reflection on the methods and principles of Aristotle and Aquinas. Thus Pope John's way to the Church's ancient tradition was made straight by contemporary philosophic labors; in *Mater et Magistra* he states explicitly that the Holy See's social doctrine was clarified "with the cooperation of enlightened priests and laymen, especially during the last century."

Donald R. Campion, S.J., has compiled a fascinating report[1] on nearly two-hundred studies which tried to interpret the revolutionary impact of *Mater et Magistra*. The energy of these comments and the range of their disagreements indicate the ferment and restlessness at the grassroots which the Vatican Council has crystallized for the public gaze. Nevertheless, it is not easy to apply the thinking of Pope John to the American situation. Too little work has been done here. The ideas leading up to the encyclicals are too new in America; the public has not been prepared for Pope John's imperatives.

The American Catholic people in general seem still to be

[1] Cf. the collection by Justus George Lawler and Joseph N. Moody, *The Challenge of Mater et Magistra* (Herder and Herder, 1963).

living in the world of Latin Scholasticism; they leave initiative to their clergy, attend their devotions and private
duties, and are unaware of Christian imperatives toward
"the reconstruction of the social order." Fr. Campion cites
a Roman visitor to America after the publication of *Mater
et Magistra*, who noted that, on the American Catholic
scene, "the challenge to papal authority in social matters"
comes not from the left but from the right. But then, American pulpits have been largely silent about the social encyclicals of Leo XIII, Pius XI, and the messages of Pius XII.
Thus it is no wonder that the American secular community
regards American Catholics as politically and socially self-
ish and unenlightened.

This same secular community, on the other hand, recognizes the selflessness and moral leadership of Pope John.
The New York *Times* has outdone itself in praising him
and supporting him. Why can secular thinkers understand
what he is saying? Pope John's "fundamental principle" is
that "individual human beings are and should be the foundation, the end and the subjects of all the institutions in
which social life is carried on." The pope affirms that this
principle "guarantees the sacred dignity of the individual";
at the same time he insists that human beings are by their
nature "intrinsically social." He reconciles both longings of
men: for personal dignity and for community. The pope
is at one and the same time a twentieth-century man, and
a man steeped in the best traditions of the West: traditions
which belong, ultimately, to the entire race.

This is why Pope John can address all men of good will,

and be relevant to their deepest concerns. In the Anglo-American world, for example, several important philosophers are moving away from the simpler forms of utilitarian ethics, toward a new emphasis upon the uniqueness of the human person. They could easily support the pope's "fundamental principle." In a textbook widely used on secular campuses, for instance, Richard B. Brandt defends an analysis of ethical terms and a method for resolving ethical disputes, the "Qualified Attitude Method," which is very close to Aristotle's conception of prudence—far closer than Latin Scholastic manuals generally are. Henry David Aiken, influenced by European existentialists, seems also to be moving away from impersonal British empiricism toward an analysis of those factors in ethical judgment and decision which are at once personal and objective.

But the most important move in the Anglo-American tradition in this connection is that taken by John Rawls in his often-cited article, "Justice as Fairness." Professor Rawls, who lectures in ethics at Harvard, objects to utilitarianism because it takes the stance in ethics of the executive-administrator, and does not sufficiently respect the personal factors in ethical decisions. He argues that to represent our ethical convictions accurately, at least one new premise must be added to classical utilitarianism, viz., that no one may justify an inequality simply because the disadvantages of those on one side are outweighed by the advantages of those on the other. This premise rules out mere technical calculations, and insists on personal dignity. Rawls follows Aristotle in taking the equal rights of persons as the basis of

fairness, and in taking fairness rather than utilitarian calculation as basic to the conception of justice. If this move
by Rawls is widely accepted, British empiricism will have
taken a major step toward a conception of the person shared
by Pope John.

If Anglo-American philosophy is moving toward an existential conception of natural law, based on the conditions
which any person must meet in order to justify his ethical
judgments, Pope John is restoring to Catholic teaching its
similar emphasis on the integrity of the individual person
in his historical situation. In *Pacem in terris*, he upholds
the right of each man to worship God "according to the
dictates of an upright conscience." He makes perfectly explicit later in the encyclical (against certain Scholastics)
that "error" does not deprive a person of his rights or of his
dignity. Again, the pope stresses the heightened consciousness which men in our times have of their rights; this evolution of consciousness, he argues, at last makes effective
a morality of human equality. Finally, in the passage on
cooperation of Catholics with non-Catholics, the pope instructs Catholics to distinguish "philosophic teachings"
from "historical movements." The former, "once they are
drawn up and defined, remain always the same," the latter
"working in historical situations in constant evolution" are
"subject to changes even of a profound nature." He thus
brings the secret of Anglo-American political cooperation
into the teaching of the Church universal.

Pope John's moral perspective, therefore, is not abstract,
essentialistic, utopian. It is historical and concrete. It calls

to mind, in many points of methodology and emphasis, the viewpoint of Maritain's *Humanisme Intégral,* which is too little read by Anglo-American philosophers. In its emphasis on historical existence and the individual person, Pope John's viewpoint is a decisive break with Latin Scholasticism. Where the pope emphasizes persons, the Latin Scholastic emphasizes ideological position. Where the pope emphasizes the evolution of political and social consciousness, the Latin Scholastic emphasizes eternal definitions. Pope John is a political realist in the tradition of Aristotle and Aquinas; he is neither an idealist of eternal forms nor a pragmatist of immediate expedience. His vision is too compromising for the former and too futuristic for the latter.

Nevertheless, it must be admitted that in these two major encyclicals Pope John has poured his new wine in old skins: his moral vision strains the Scholastic terminology he uses, rupturing it in places, held back by it in others. He still uses the image of a law "written on the hearts" of men, though Dom Odon Lottin has shown that this image, far from being Aquinan, belongs to the Platonic tradition against which Aquinas labored. The pope is fond of traditional phrases like "principles which are universal, absolute, and unchangeable," even in contexts in which he has been arguing that men have come only gradually to consciousness of many of their rights. There is thus a marked tension in these encyclicals between the static and the dynamic, the essentialistic and the historical.

This tension is indicative of the struggle still going on

within the Church. Pope John has introduced the victories won by Emmanuel Mounier, Maritain, Gabriel Marcel, Teilhard de Chardin, Lonergan and others, into the most authoritative ordinary teaching of the Church. But these victories were won while many in high posts and low remained in the eternal, absolute, unchanging fortresses of Latin Scholasticism. To make himself understood, Pope John has seemed to use the familiar forms, the familiar words, though his vision is not Scholastic. On the other hand, his vision has deep roots in the existential, historical Aristotelian tradition, in the Aristotle of the *Ethics* and the *Politics*.

Thus, it is self-defeating to turn the modern polemic against Scholasticism into an attack on the Western philosophical tradition, as the advocates of modern Scripture studies and liturgical reform are wont to do. The use of the words "kerygmatic," "Hebrew rather than Greek," and even Pope John's "pastoral," are in a way evasions. They are obviously and explicitly directed against the viewpoint of Latin Scholasticism, which is abstract, categorical, unhistorical, impersonal. But to those in the Scholastic fortresses, polemic cannot fail to seem like a betrayal of tradition, an abandonment of sound philosophy. Moreover, insofar as it is merely a reaction, this polemic alienates and does not reconcile. It creates the same intellectual impasse as the revolt of existentialism against traditional rationalism or British analytic philosophy; rival camps grow up, without mutual communication. The Scholastic must be shown that modern theology is not a surrender to the existentialist, romantic *Zeitgeist*. On the contrary, he must be shown that it is he who is standing far outside the authentic tradition, high and dry on a Platonic island, out of the stream of the Church's life.

But the question that seems to worry the conservative is how he—and the Church with him—can have been wrong for so many years. Can the infallible Church have been unfaithful to herself? One can sympathize very well with the sense of panic and loss the Latin Scholastics seem to feel as the waves of history erode their island; won't the Church disappear, indistinguishable from secular currents? This fear is at the root of the condemnation of Modernism and the recent innuendoes of heresy against the new theology. The "closed door" school wants dikes against the floods, to preserve the identity of the Church.

Moreover, the reformers do not seem to realize the gravity of the changes they are bringing about. Whereas, before, the words "eternal, absolute, unchanging" gave security and one had only to turn to the Curia for a clarification, now it is becoming impossible to take anything for granted. Attitudes toward Protestants, Jews, Orthodox, and most recently the Communists, have been revolutionized. There has not been, of course, any compromise "in principle." But is this saving phrase any more than rhetoric? Has not the Church in fact and in the presence of actual men given up her pretensions to unchanging spiritual authority?

Between the compromises of pragmatism and the rigidity

of eternal truth, the conservatives do not see the Aristotelian synthesis. Furthermore, it is exactly these two alternatives between which their own teaching and practice oscillate. There is nothing more striking about Latin Scholasticism than its doctrine of "prudence," by whose rubric it is often ruthless and unscrupulous in action, while professing eternal values untarnished by the claims of the human situation. Latin politics work by the same dichotomy; the Latin will die to proclaim eternal truths, whose abuse in practice he tolerates with a shrug.

The "eternal truths" of which Pope John speaks are not the sort that are written as definitions "beyond the firmament." They are, rather, the sort of verity William Faulkner spoke of in his memorable acceptance speech on receiving the Nobel Prize: founded not in definitions but in that physical and emotional and only partly rational organism: man in history. Ambition and lust, love and sacrifice, pride and passion recur because man cannot escape his origin, limitations, or history. It is in this sense only that there is a "natural law," progressively made clear in history, never quite complete, always affected by the continuing dialogue between God and His people down the generations. Thus Pope John's list of natural rights was not evident, in theory or in practice, when the Gospels were first preached, nor, indeed, in the thirteenth or even in the nineteenth century. It is difficult to formulate even a single "principle of natural law" which has not come to be recognized only gradually through history, and which has not under certain conditions been permitted: even "thou shalt not kill," or torture prisoners, or have slaves.

Thus the use of the words "absolute," "unchanging," "eternal," must be taken in a limited, special sense. From God's point of view, man's nature may lie limpid and apparent, and revelation may help to fix some of these insights for finite men. But from an empirical human point of view, men learn the natural law only gradually and according to the lessons of history. Pope John has succeeded in returning the Church to this ancient perspective. Against the advice of the "prophets of doom," he has returned Catholicism to the world. He has cast the Church free from the island of Latin Scholasticism on which she has for some centuries been marooned, and launched her once more on the currents of human history with hope, with courage, with joy, with the exhilaration proper to those who see in the darkness the star of eternal life. So doing, he made it possible for Catholics to speak of good news to their companions who do not see, and to learn from those who do not see, the humility of the human situation.

PART TWO

THE EDUCATION OF THE
NEW GENERATION

7 THE GAP
BETWEEN INTELLECTUALS
AND PEOPLE

A man who loses his roots in the people, Dostoevsky once wrote, will soon become an atheist. His insight has been borne out in American history. But Dostoevsky neglected to add that the wider the gap between intellectuals and people, the more ineffectual, insensitive, and superficial religion soon becomes. The prejudices and narrowness of religious people drive the most sensitive and alert of the young farther from their roots. The vicious circle becomes increasingly hard to stop. Thus, the most urgent problem faced by the new generation is the split between the general Catholic culture of America and the secular intellectual culture. This problem sets the major obstacle its education must meet. It will be worth our while to dwell first on the general cultural problem, and then on the secular universities, the Catholic schools, and the public schools. We will also reflect on related cultural issues, especially on the conflict between the technical and the human.

"A large, oval head, smooth, faceless, unemotional, but

a little bit haughty and condescending . . . superficial in approach to any problem . . . a doctrinaire supporter of Middle-European socialism . . . a bleeding heart." So John Alsop and Louis Bromfield explained the new word of 1952, "egg-head." The people of America did not resist the word; it seemed to fit their fears and resentments. It illustrated the gap between them and the liberal intellectuals, the gap which rendered both ineffective, and crippled mid-century America. Perhaps the Presidency of John F. Kennedy will narrow it—among Roman Catholics, who have been among the most conservative and those most suspicious of the intellectuals. What caused this split between the two groups in American society? When did it occur?

The success of liberal ideas under Franklin D. Roosevelt and Harry Truman was too gratifying to be deep. Hunger and hardship forced the people to try Roosevelt in 1932; the depression gave him his mandate, the war helped keep him in. It is not so clear why Harry Truman won, but in two terms under the popular Eisenhower the Republicans could not even suggest repealing liberal programs. This does not mean that the American people have been deeply liberalized; they have maintained large reservations about liberal reasoning and analyses. Roman Catholics seem a case in point. Ordinarily Democratic, lower middle class, and hit hard by the depression, they were among the most ardent supports of F.D.R. But they never shared whole-heartedly the ideologic drift of liberalism, its sympathies with the Soviet experiment, its more or less relativist ethic and its sometimes mere tolerance of religion (or positive enmity). Under the pressures of industrialized society, of big and impersonal business, of ruthless laws of boom and recession, the American people could, however, turn to the liberal intellectual leadership of Roosevelt. In him, the reform movements of seventy years crystallized into national action, and the people were for the first time mobilized behind them. But it must not be thought that the people accepted the ideologies from which these movements sprang. The people accepted leadership, as in a nonideological democracy they should, on a pragmatic basis. They maintained a reservoir of suspicion and perhaps of fear.

The liberal intellectual seems to have been misled by the popularity of Roosevelt, and all the more so by the surprising victory of Harry Truman in 1948. Perhaps the Second World War and the Korean War kept his attention elsewhere; perhaps America is simply too large and diverse a country, and her people too varying in political sophistication; but the liberal intellectual has not been noticeably self-critical in his success, nor deft in bringing the people to understand just what he was doing. For many years there was almost no such thing as a conservative intellectual; the books, reviews and journals read in intellectually respectable circles were all by liberals; Mencken, Babbitt, More and a scattering of others were influential but somehow peripheral. And it is hard to be a conservative in a country that lives so much in the future as does America, that was given a fresh starting place as though outside the ugly tangles of history, that was created by rational decision for rational goals ahead in the future. As a result, when the liberal is not self-critical, there has been almost no force to check him and make him revise his positions. His unchallenged self-esteem nourishes in others fears and resentments whose release in the "egghead" epithet is sudden and virulent.

Lack of self-criticism is not good for a liberal intellectual, either. The ugly "red herring" trials, the communist assault on Korea, then Hungary, marked an ever more complete end to innocence. The liberal intellectual had been wrong about the Soviets, not entirely but significantly. On the home scene, national crime syndicates have been thriving for a generation; juvenile delinquency resists solution; the national moral sense seems to be growing ever less certain —perhaps, it must be admitted, as much because of welfare programs as because of free-enterprise emphasis on consumer goods; perhaps as much because of the relativist ethics of the schools as because of the *simpliste*, emotional ethics of the preachers. When the liberal intellectual in the person of Adlai Stevenson tried to "talk sense" to the American people, he found himself no longer uncompromised. The liberal intellectual was not looked upon as representing political and moral wisdom. He had gone many years without self-criticism, without inner revision, without intensifying his contact with the moral sense of the people. Americans looked to Ike for integrity.

But neither was Eisenhower self-critical. For eight years America did not live a life of truth, but a life of comfort.

Eisenhower could not understand how wrong this was; in his mind it seemed to be of the essence to "keep up the spirits of the troops," to "keep up morale." But a democracy does not run on comfort, it runs on rational criticism or on nothing. John Kennedy campaigned on the theme of rational awakening, and he won the election. The thin margin of victory seems to indicate, among other things, how much the people do not accept many of the liberal presuppositions, much of the liberal world view. Events force them to the liberal camp, because the liberals at least promise action. But the association is not restful and at ease.

Why isn't the relationship between liberal intellectual and people more cordial than it is? Most of the blame, I fear, must fall upon the intellectual, for he is the one whose mind is supposed to be more universal, and therefore more able to communicate from one set of ideas and words into another. And surely it is obvious that words have different emotional charges in different groups; that the people do not spontaneously take the point of view of the trained mind, or the historical perspective of the omnivorous reader. The people do not analyze events or changed situations; they go on living, they suffer and are happy, in turn. They are as they are: there, a fact. There is no need to romanticize them, or to despair of them; they pass judgment upon their leaders. They have a certain shrewdness, an inchoate sense of traditional history, a responsiveness that is a mixture of the rational and the irrational. Yet the critical, rational working of democracy depends on increasing, as far as possible, the proportion of the rational to the irrational in their activity. The mere projection of an image by a prospective leader is important in winning an election; but mutual rational criticism between leaders and people is indispensable in the realization of policy. The liberal intellectual must learn rational communication with the people, for his own good and for theirs.

There are several obstacles to this communication. One of these is on the side of the people, others on the side of the liberal intellectual. The people's primary concern is to live, not to reflect; this is their weakness, and their strength. While ideologies and interpretations of history come and go, the people go on living. But they live in a kind of darkness, and they are often the victims of their own lack of reflection. They remain attached to a pattern of life that is no longer viable; or they suffer from new patterns which they do not understand well enough to create machinery to change. They depend on their intellectuals to enlighten them and thus enable them to act. Yet they themselves are not utterly devoid of their own kind of wisdom, and in a democracy they pass judgment even on their superiors. In modern America, they depended on F.D.R. to interpret the cause of their economic helplessness, and to give them the means to fight back. But, as I have suggested, the liberals who engineered the New Deal did not succeed in thinking through and in communicating to the people the presuppositions of what they were doing, its justification and its salient effects. They were content to meet the concrete crisis, and they were rejoiced by success. The ideological springs of their reforms had century-old roots, were colored by European origins and specific European developments in the nineteenth century. But in the concrete tasks of effecting the New Deal, in the war and postwar period, there was not time to think through the differences between American reality and European reality.

America is not Europe. Freedom is not the same as the French *liberté*. Our free enterprise (a misnomer in itself) is not *Das Kapital*. Our democracy is not an ideological *État enseignant*. Our people are not the proletariat of Marx, nor "the masses" of D. H. Lawrence and many others on the Continent. Our liberty under law does not oppose law to liberty in the fashion of Roman and Napoleonic law, or in the fashion of Latin revolutionaries. The liberal intellectual of America has often failed to grasp our newness, our difference, our identity. Parrington's *Main Currents of American Thought*, for example, is an interpretation of American reality in a viewpoint borrowed from European ideology, and it is not alone. Again, the 1960 debate in *Life* and in the *New York Times* on America's National Purpose revealed that in these liberal years we seem to have forgotten our purpose, and our identity, in the very midst of liberal reforms and a major war. A European aura has hung about the programs of the liberal intellectual in America, while often he has in his heart rejected America. He has been ashamed of American civilization. He has surely not discovered her riches of the spirit. He flays her with negative criticism. He does not release the unused idealism and energies of a people unique upon the globe for their hope in reason and in generosity.

The liberal intellectual has despised the kingdom of supermarkets and organization. He has despised the blind quest for profits and for prestige, and the directing of the behemoth of technology toward surfeit of consumer goods. He has decried the using of men as parts in the machine of economic process. Above all, he has held in contempt the dedication of the public-relations men of industry, government and even the churches, to the comfortable falsehood and the optimistic pretense. He has grown to hate the affable smile. The people of America do not realize the depth of the sea of lies in which they are forced to live; and while, spontaneously, they do not believe what they hear, they yet, unreflecting, do not rise up in revolt or truth, or even sympathize with those who try to tell the truth. They go on living as if it were an expected part of life to share the huge cultural lie: that to keep smiling will see one through. But the liberal intellectual also does not see that *he* helped start all this, that back in the beginning it was his Enlightenment that conceived the idea of the rationalization of society. It was his Enlightenment that conceived of the new purpose of civilization as the bringing of maximum contentment to the greatest number by concrete changes in the *environment*. The men of the Enlightenment said that "Knowledge is power," and they made the discoveries and the inventions that made the technological revolution possible. It was their optimism that communicated itself to the thrust of our civilization.

Thus in his contempt for the mass culture and the barbaric Philistines he knows it can breed, the liberal intellectual sometimes forgets his own contribution to the making of our present world. Further, in turning away from the ugly aspects of the American economic system, the liberal intellectual does not always succeed in removing the colored glasses of European ideology. He has rarely tried to understand the American business world for what it is, its human achievements and virtues as well as its dehumanization. And now Europe is exhausted and looks to the American intellectual for light; the uncommitted nations look here for persuasion. The American intellectual is embarrassed by his own scathing rejections of his culture, and his little sympathy for the whole area of it—the area of *technique*—in which most of the people live out their lives. He has not seen what Henry Ford's revolution has done for the lives and spirit of the people, though he approved Roosevelt's protection of the people from the huge, impersonal forces of centralized business. The business system of America contributes to the welfare of the human spirit, as well as takes its toll of it; I can think of no system, in history or in the realm of ideas, that has not shared this ambiguity. Its great fault is its impersonal domination over men, the absence of personal intelligence and will directing it. The liberal intellectuals need to create new forms which would give thrust to the human spirit's need to master technology. Even in its present form, however, the American political-economic system is unique and perhaps uniquely human. It does not have unique expression or adequate image whereby it might be communicated to the understanding of other peoples. The liberal intellectual image of America is not adequate; neither is the image proposed by the business community. What other is there?

The people of America do not understand the changes that have come over our land in the last fifty years. Their heads are full of images of the frontier, of the familial and old-fashioned virtues; or else full of distress because these things are passing away. The civic virtues needed for our present life are quite different from those of two generations ago; the economic and international forces that control our lives are greater, and our need to work together is more critical. The set of virtues to which Barry Goldwater appeals is not a false set; it is simply not adequate. Our enemies and tasks are different from those our forebears faced. Agrarian virtues are different from the urban and sub-urban; they are not better or worse. The call to manhood still is the call to responsible judgment and courageous will, and only the individual can answer this call; though surely now the field for answering it is that of cooperation and not that of rugged individualism. Big business, central-ized as nothing else in the world, and its counterweight, big government, are not perfect arrangements, but they are what we must live with, and they call for new sets of political and moral skills.

The liberal intellectual has not eased for the people this transition to a new way of life. The *avant garde* has sometimes despised the people it was supposed to be leading; the beats, too, sneer at the squares. Sometimes the liberal intellectual has not understood genuine religion, and has tended to think of all religion as superstition, quite its opposite. Thus he has not in such cases been able to respect the religious virtues of many noble and heroic families among the people; he has also been cut off from one of the sources of energy in Western civilization—though there are, of course, many liberals who have not cut themselves off from these sources. Again, the liberal ethic has tended to be relativist. Even the extremities of the National Socialists were difficult for him to condemn intellectually, for the standard of morality had become more a matter of the sensibilities and of an undefined sense of honor than of the intelligence; the Nazis had acted for "the good of the state," hadn't they? In making fun of the bourgeois virtues, and in exposing the mechanisms of misdirected fears of sex, the liberal intellectual has once more moved out in front of the moral sense of the people, and not made the transition of the people to the new insights easy. The people have often thought the liberal intellectual amoral or even immoral, and the liberal intellectual has often thought the people benighted and stupid. Both groups, however, often share a deep moral sense, though its direction and expression differ in each.

Meanwhile, the emergence of communism as a world power has dramatized moral issues that have always lain at the root of society, but which have not always been so clear. The evils of capitalistic civilization, of both European and American type, favor the moral thrust of communism; but the unscrupulousness of communism destroys morality in the very name of justice. The cold war is not a war that can be "won" or "lost" in the usual sense; even so, it becomes harder and harder to reconcile oneself to the notion that ideas and systems make no difference, that all is relative, that good intentions are enough. If the cold war endures without military mishap and indefinitely, then the force of opposite moral ideas will become increasingly important. The destruction of the Iron Curtain is the first condition for this interaction of ideas, but the destruction of our own Emotional Curtain of suspicion and of fear is the second. As long as both sides hide from the level of reason, we shall be in constant peril—even if neither side wanted mutual destruction, but had no way of communicating with the other, the unreasonable would inevitably happen.

But even if these curtains are heaved up and rational communication is opened, what shall the liberal intellectual of America say to the world? He is not a salesman. He is not a public-relations man. He is not a mouther of virtuous phrases, nor a cataloguer of the excellences of his own people. His task is to grasp the lines of the emerging interacting consciousness of mankind. The pivot of all future development, the arrowhead of advance, is what happens in men's individual consciousness, a consciousness increasingly informed by currents from all around the world, a consciousness increasingly in communion with that of other men. East and West will disintegrate; humanity will emerge. This is the long-term struggle, of which the present is the springtime.

The development of rational consciousness, among individuals and in the world as a whole, is the line of advance. Beyond emotions, beyond prejudices, beyond reflexes, lie intelligent self-possession and integrity of will. The liberal intellectual in America must open the way to this advance first among his own people, then the peoples of the non-committed world, and the peoples of the hostile world. He must understand what it is about American business that has given the lie to Marxian analysis and robbed that analysis of the fulfillment of its predictions in America, and indeed in Western Europe. He must also grasp the intellectual-moral change that comes over the general populace of those nations that move from an agrarian to an urban culture, its contributions to the human spirit as well as its penalties. He must grasp the ill effects of the welfare state, as of big business, upon the human spirit, and devise checks and balances there as elsewhere. He must cease thinking in the vaguely Socialist forms of the last seventy years, and the vaguely Utopian forms of the modern centuries, as if the contentment of the greatest number and not the development of rational consciousness were the goal of civilization. New energies of spirit are needed in our generation, new means of liberating intelligence and courage.

The liberal intellectual, then, must learn to criticize

himself, to widen his sense of values by engaging himself in the not perfect but actual American culture, and he must open a way for the American people to a fuller grasp of the possibilities of the present for the human spirit. He cannot communicate with the people by scorning what the people hold dear, nor by repeating presuppositions the people do not share and cannot understand without teachers possessed of empathy and infinite concern. If the liberal doubted himself, saw the ambiguities in much that he has cherished, admitted his mistakes, ceased thinking of others as merely unenlightened, he would be much more ready for leadership to a new world order. The fusion of the ideals of the people with the ideals of the liberal intellectuals, and perhaps of genuine religious traditions with the traditions of the Enlightenment, would create a cultural force of great power. It might be sufficient to drive the overlords of falsehood from Madison Avenue and Hollywood, and free the genius of America for its worldwide tasks. This fusion must begin in the schools.

8 GOD IN THE COLLEGES

The most critical battlefront for the human person lies on the university campus and in the classrooms of the schools. At present, education in America is not for persons, but for technicians. Young men and women go to school to obtain the equipment for getting a job and attaining success in life. A tactical battle rages between some scientists and some protagonists of the liberal arts over educational theory. The former want an education more technical still, founded on the discipline of scientific method and ruthless with the obscurantist educational traditions of the past. The protagonists of the liberal arts are less clear about their aims. They, too, believe that knowledge is power, and in most of their disciplines they take pains to imitate scientific procedures as rigorously as they can. Unless they are romantics, appealing to certain feelings and intuitions which "escape" science, they share roughly, and in the main, the same epistemology as the scientists: knowledge is for prediction and control. To watch a literary critic at work is, generally, to watch an "objective observer," who brings technical equipment to a work that remains "out there" apart from himself. He may speak of Tolstoi, Flaubert, Dostoevsky, Camus—like Lane in Salinger's *Franny and Zooey*—but he is no more like them as a man than the man in the moon. The protagonist of the liberal arts has become as much a technician as the scientist; we only rarely and by accident educate persons in America.

Moreover, the treadmill on which our students are expected to take their place at graduation deadens criticism and creativity. American culture governs American schools; they are, perhaps, among the least free in the world. The environment pollutes their atmosphere; the same climb to success, the same petty prejudices, the same imperceptive attitudes mark the campuses as mark the businesses and professions in the towns. The academies lay claim to superiority, which they seldom seem to attain. They turn students back to their home towns with nearly the same prejudices, interests, and habits as they had when they came to school. The quality of political debate in America is so low, vulgar, and inadequate that one must question why education (as we now have it) is essential to democracy: What does it add to the natural man? Where are numbers of Americans, small but proportionate to the great numbers of those who go to college, who read with discrimination? who understand *both* sides of an argument? who appreciate painting, music, and drama and support them in their localities? who have by habit the Socratic or religious passion for personal and social reform?

The reason for the apathy in American life is that too

many Americans feel like instruments, like tools, like technicians so complex that machines have not yet—not yet—been developed to replace them. Their education encourages this feeling. They are supposed to become "useful" members of society, to make a "useful" contribution to humanity. Their education does not touch them as persons, but as tools. It is carried out at a degree of abstraction which is largely irrelevant to them, unless they want to fit into the system and "succeed." Most of their education is so remote it could, as B. F. Skinner urges, be carried out better by machines. Its twisted notion of "objectivity" is destructive. Its methods of testing, by true-false and multiple-choice questionnaires, are contemptible substitutes for complex personal reflection. It favors the intelligent manipulator of words, the organism quickest to pick up the signals of the leading or the local culture circle. If we wish to continue to educate such technicians and such reactors, perhaps we should take Professor Skinner rigorously; he has grasped the logic of our situation. Teaching machines do the same work as our present teachers, only more efficiently. Boston, New York, Chicago, Los Angeles, and the small towns in between are becoming as alike as Walden Two, and Three, and Four, only less logically.

Men, however, are persons as well as technicians. Besides needing to do the world's work, they need to discover themselves. Besides the kind of knowing useful for predicting and controlling, they need the kind of knowing, indirect and reflective, by which the command of Socrates is heeded: Know thyself. More than they need to possess things, they need to come to know and to appropriate themselves—to find themselves in the mazes of ignorance, passion, and self-illusion which hide them from themselves. They need to know that each of them is unique and irreplaceable, not for what he has or can do, not for his fame or position or general usefulness, but for what he is. Being is more important to a man, though harder to attain, than having. To have takes only skill and cunning, or birth, or luck. To become what one is capable of becoming takes an arduous search for the unknown—the unknown, not any one—a long discipline against impulse and prejudice and self-deception, and great reserves of courage against long, or sudden, opposition. Many Americans have; few seem to be. Many are restless and discontent. In their eyes one can sometimes see a question difficult to voice: What have I lost? What turn in the road was a mistake? If Americans are guilty, it is not so much for deeds as for a way of life.

To become a person is not easy. The task needs all the resources of education. Unless there are persons, moreover, faith in God is meaningless. The shallowness of American religion is largely due the style of American education, as an example may make clear.

A philosophy professor once asked his class: "How many of you believe in the existence of God?" The class was intellectually alive and usually argued, but as he walked up and down no hands went up.

"Good," he said. "Then I'll give you Anselm's proof for the existence of God." In a few minutes, he had presented the proof. "Now," he paused. "How many of you see anything wrong in this proof?" No hands went up. "Well," he said, "then some of you now believe in the existence of God. How many?"

Still no hands went up, of course. The students knew it was an academic exercise. In telling about it later, the professor shrugged: "What can you do when thinking doesn't seem to make any difference?"

In the colleges, the life of personal conviction is quite separate from the life of academic intelligence. The academy is make-believe, and does not often touch the person. This part of the phenomenon is not confined to America; it is well known in England: in *Lucky Jim*, Kingsley Amis mocks the noncommitment, sham, and hollowness in middle-class education. But the phenomenon is especially acute in America. Vladimir Nabokov burlesques the American college in *Pnin*. John K. Galbraith's *The Affluent Society* describes the emergence of the new and numerous educated middle class which dominates the horizons of our generation.

How does God fare in a middle-class education? What happens to religion in the middle-class world view? Since medieval times the West has been becoming middle class. Concomitantly it has witnessed the rise of technology. Social and economic changes made Europe capitalist, then industrialist; the world view of the West has changed as well. Even though the bourgeoisie might cling to the conventions and forms of an older tradition and an older faith, the impersonality of business and the objectivity of scientific method were molding their weekday spirits and their habitual attitudes. The very bourgeoisie that nourished the technological and scientific revolution, nourished within itself an intellectual avant–garde that strove to point out to it how very empty its forms had become. The avant garde was usually increasingly irreligious: from Voltaire and Hume, Comte, and Zola, to Shaw and Russell, it has come to take its battle vis-à-vis religion as won. For its point has been that our culture is now at base irreligious, that the bourgeois businessman who pretends differently is either hypocritical or blind. Catholicism was long content with the status quo, and Protestantism for a long time praised the thrifty and the rugged and the strong. Thus the war on poverty which Marxism declared and which the democracies have taken up is (though it need not have been) a secular war, and the ideals which international civilization now pursue are secular ideals: the abolition of poverty and disease, of ignorance and indignity, of colonialism and tyranny. Giving itself to science and technology, our culture makes religion not central but optional, and the avant garde has been trying to point out—and to form—the change.

Secondly, it is necessary to see that while Europe was torn nearly to its death by the ideological and physical contortions of recent revolutions and wars, America and England have tried earnestly to go on as before, as if nothing has happened. The war washed away the intellectual foundations of Europe's past, and intellectuals like Camus, Sartre, Marcel, Barth, and Guardini have fought desperately for intellectual starting points—whether they deny or affirm the possibility of religious faith. But in America and England, philosophy and art showed little such desperation; men tried to pick up where they had left off, a little more tired, a little more angry, worried about the bomb, but not fundamentally changed. Moreover, education in England and America has become financially cushioned as never before. The government, corporations, unions—all give grants for specialized research or simply for the maintenance of students and professors. A distinctly comfortable and entrenched kind of existence is growing up. The small, modestly optimistic world view which Europe shared before the wars is still almost possible. The radicalism of the American thirties has been fragmented by prosperity and by disillusion with ideology.

Although the colleges pride themselves on the awakening of young minds, on the asking of the Big Questions of life (who and what is man? whence has he come? where is he going? what is love? what is passion? what is reason? is there a God?), it is soon clear to college students that the Big Questions don't count—either in academic standing, or in later life, or in research grants.

In the first place, the standing assumption is that ultimate questions are in principle unanswerable, and hence not worth asking seriously. This assumption may not discourage freshmen, but over a four-year period it is pretty well driven home. In the second place, nobody is much interested in students' answers to such questions, or deems them worth putting in competition with anybody else's. Even among the professors it is assumed that ultimate questions are nonintellectual, personal, and if matters of supreme importance and self-commitment, nevertheless not matters for passionate academic dispute. The university, on principle, concentrates on statistics, historical facts, historical intellectual positions, logic modeled on the discourse of the physical sciences, and ample documentation. Even the literature courses, under the impact of the New Criticism, have the students noting the occurences of words, running down allusions, and abstracting from the conditions of history. The Anglo-American university has committed itself to all that is "objective," countable, precise, publicly verifiable. Though this commitment suits the middle-class temper capitally, it stifles religion almost to death.

Not only religion is stifled. More fundamentally, it is possible—it is even common—for a student to go to class after class of sociology, economics, psychology, literature, philosophy, and the rest, and hardly become aware that he is dealing with issues of life and death, of love and solitude, of inner growth and pain. He may never fully grasp the fact that education is not so much information and technique as self-confrontation and change in his own

conscious life. He may sit through lectures and write ex-
aminations—and the professors may let him do merely
that—collecting verbal "answers," without really thinking
through and deciding about any new aspect of his own
life in any course. The dilemma of education has always
been to combine merely mental skills with personal ex-
periencing and growth. The educational currents in American colleges tend to oscillate from one pole to the other;
and at present the attention in college to the formal and
the public easily leaves the inner life of the student un-
touched.

It is true that in a place like Harvard, or among more
serious students everywhere, the young collegian may experience beneficial crises of growth. He gets a taste of
rebellion against his origins; he may become, for a while,
avant–garde. The folks at home find him restive, critical,
hostile, in his approach to a world he had hitherto peace-
fully shared. He has learned to despise the organization man
and the many patterns of conformity in mass culture; he
has learned a certain contempt for suburbia and its values.
Yet he likes the comforts of home. Worst of all, in college
he has not really had to rebel (except perhaps against not
having Latin on his diploma). The college gave him rebellious, critical books, but also gave him a cool grove to
read them in. No commitment, no crusading, no heroism
is asked of him. The college merely wants him to "have
the facts," to show mental control of the concepts. Yet he,
so everyone tells him, is not at all like the collegians of the

thirties, or even of the forties. He is cautious, quiet, studious. And no wonder. So is the institution in which he is studying. The higher-powered institutions are committed to testable information and techniques; the patterns of conformity in lower-powered institutions do not far transcend the interests of the society that fosters them.

Middle-class Christianity—the bourgeois Christianity which Nietzsche, Kierkegaard, Péguy, Bloy, and others so hated—was always prudent, small-visioned, secure. It dared little, with its gaudy-colored plaster statues, or its devices to protect the little world of the entrepreneur. In the person of many university professors, middle-class secular humanism is not much more daring. It thinks of itself as humble in its agnosticism, and eschews the "mystic flights" of metaphysicians, theologians, and dreamers; it is cautious and remote in dealing with heightened and passionate experiences that are the stuff of much great literature and philosophy. It limits itself to this world and its concerns, concerns which fortunately turn out to be largely subject to precise formulation, and hence have a limited but comforting certainty. (It has a particularly comfortable ambiance if it works within the physical sciences, or mathematics, or the statistics of sociology and economics.) If we cannot control the great uncertain questions in the universe, nevertheless we can make a universe of little certainties we can control.

The agnosticism—atheism would be too strong a word—

of the classroom is not militant. It is only, in principle, un-concerned. It is bourgeois Christianity all over again, to so great an extent that, in college, in spite of differences in belief, the behavior of agnostic and of religious man is pretty much the same.

The agnosticism of the classroom does not have to be militant. Once upon a time it was fighting for its life; now it is an accepted part of the college scene, in fact the pre-dominating part. The old battles between positive science and religion which delighted, or angered, our grandfathers —about chance and design, monkeys and Adam—seldom resound now in academic halls. The distinction between empirical and theological activity seems pretty well recog-nized—each side preserves a certain calm and only occasion-ally do tempers flare. Perhaps psychologists more than others are given to writing off religion as illusion; anthro-pologists, in turn, are habituated to data on revelations and recurrent religious themes, and correspondingly casual about the traditions of Judaism and Christianity. One school of analysis in philosophy, of which Russell and Ayer among others are examples, believes that nothing that cannot be reduced to sense experience can have meaning, and most religious questions of course lie outside this restricted zone. Some partisans of another movement, linguistic analysis, following the later Wittgenstein, do not require the dis-course of faith and theology to conform to other kinds of discourse, but study it in its own right; but religion does not lie in words.

Professional disciplines aside, a bland tolerance seems to be everybody's ideal. Say nothing that will offend. Say nothing that involves personal commitment. Stay close to the public facts. "You've got to teach these youngsters to forget the *shoulds* and *musts* they came here with," one new teaching fellow was recently admonished by his program director. "The students have to learn to be objective." And of course such a critique is excellent, since some *shoulds* and *musts* are what a man dies for. But there seems to be correspondingly little concern about which ones he will acquire and keep.

One Harvard professor was quoted as saying, with perhaps a touch of irony, "*Veritas* means we are committed to nothing." It may be that the American consensus has forced a "commitment to nothing" upon our universities; we are a pluralist people, and it seems very difficult to discover a way to teach about those differences on ultimate questions that make us so. The colleges make a "commitment to noncommitment," have a "faith in nonfaith." They demand perpetual re-examination and have nowhere to rest.

Thus the new middle-class tolerance of the colleges neither destroys—nor transforms—the religion of the incoming freshmen. Of one hundred students who marked themselves "atheistic or agnostic" on the poll of the Harvard *Crimson* in 1959, only ten felt "obliged . . . to enlighten others to abandon their faith." The new tolerance merely establishes, officially and in principle, that personal conviction be separated from teaching and learning. If a student wishes to commit himself to answers to ultimate questions (by commitment to some personal synthesis, or to traditional religion or ethics, or anything), he may do so—is even encouraged to do so—but not publicly, not officially, not in his daily work. He will do well to keep his answers to himself. In term papers and on tests they will not be welcome; there he is obliged to prove rather that he knows facts and correlations, and can run, seeking, as well as anyone else. No one in *official* university life seems to care about his convictions.

There is good reason for the university's position. One of its tasks is to turn out professional men. Think of the difficulty there would be in correcting exams and term papers if each student were engaged in a highly personal way in working out a position important to himself. What if the student found that something of importance to him was of minor importance to the course—or outside its confines? The dilemma of professionalism versus full human experience is a pressing one, and cannot be solved by making light of it.

How relevant is the dilemma to the actual church affiliations of college students? A Catholic report published in *America* (April 8, 1961) quotes Bishop Robert E. Lucey as saying: "The dangers to faith and morals are at least as great in a downtown office as on a secular campus." The national survey of *Time* magazine (1952) is cited to the same effect. "No appreciable number of defections," say Newman Club chaplains at the University of Illinois and the University of Iowa; those which do occur "result rather from weak religious background prior to college than from campus living and experiences." The Harvard *Crimson* poll I referred to earlier records a high rate of defections—40 per cent among Protestants, 25 per cent among Catholics, 12 per cent among Jews—among the 310 students who answered. But in almost every case the defection had its roots in precollege days, especially in high-school experience.

Although it is not clear what constitutes religious "strength," it is clear that if the student's faith goes through a personal trial-by-fire, that is his affair. There are few courses in critical theology, few in modern critical Biblical theory, few in the theory and practice of organized religion, to help him explicitly and formally to mature his theological intelligence. In the view of some religious men, this is a good thing; religion, after all, is not something that can be formally taught. It is a living commitment to be enkindled from person to person, a life to be lived rather than lessons to be learned. Besides, formal theological studies imply a living content of religious experience; but it is precisely this living content which in our day most men no longer possess. If religion is to enter the university, it must enter first at the most elementary level: in experience, in awareness, in slow and gradual exploration. The traditional words are not relevant to the present religious development of most men. Our times are sub-, not only post-, religious. The institutionalized forms of religion did not originate in modern life, and modern science and technology have grown up outside them; the two worlds of religion and modernity are strangers to each other. Were there to be merely formal courses in theology at the university, genuine religious life would fare hardly better than at present. As the New Criticism is to art, so is critical theology to religious awareness. Theology, like the New Criticism, has a role to play, but it is neither necessary nor sufficient for religious life.

If we admit that theologians would also contribute to the professionalism and formalism already thriving in the modern university, who might do better? The answer, I suggest, must be that the greatest contribution to the religious life of the university could come from teachers and scholars—formally religious or not—who could lead the student to the profound human experiences lying below the surface of the academic curriculum.

These experiences are often "prereligious"; they are barely starting points for full religious life. But they are the only foundation on which anything living can be built. I mean man's experience of his fragility, of his transitoriness, of his tininess; his consciousness of his uniqueness on the earth, of his endless and restless questioning; his personal choices whose motives and consequences he cannot fully know; his vast ability to be proud and to fail, to be isolated and to love, to be—and yet not to be—the master of his own destiny.

These experiences, and others like them, underlie the statistics of economics and of sociology, the laws and hypotheses of psychology, philosophy, and other disciplines;

they are at the source of great poems and novels and histories now often taught as if they were technical puzzles.

Large and unsettling personal questions arise from these experiences. And it is by their answers, explicit or implicit, that men finally differ from one another: how they react to achievement, to pride, to love, to suffering, to feelings of life and energy, to death. Implicit in the actions of every man is his own particular bias and approach to economics, to social and political affairs, to all matters with which he deals. What are the biases and beliefs that make a student unique and color all his judgments even in his professional concerns? Instead of concentrating on this question, and hence helping the student toward self-discovery, the university takes the easier path: it tries to maintain an area of "objectivity" and "fact." But the truly crucial element in human knowing (I repeat: even in professional knowing) lies in the recesses of personal judgment. Our critical sciences, unlike our creative arts, have favored the "objective" over the "subjective." Our universities favor the one pole over the necessary two: notional-verbal competence, over the self-knowledge and self-commitment that also affect professional careers, and make up personal life.

If university teachers could right the balance, would religion begin to thrive? Those who have made faith central to their lives—who believe in the reality and relevance of God, and the interaction (in dark faith) of God and men—hold that it would. And if theology, as such, came to the campuses and became there embattled and truly controversial, this would be welcome; for the very fact that fundamental questions were posed would transform the experience of university life.

No one can know what the full consequences of such a transformation might be, but surely it would mean that university people would be far more closely engaged with the world outside than they are today. Religious men in colleges could follow the example of the clergymen who took part in the Freedom Rides, went to jail, went on a hunger strike in the name of justice and brotherly concern. Religion has played a large role in the commitment of the young Negroes to struggle for their rights. It must suggest *other* ways of acting when situations in our society call for justice and compassion and protest. Religious men must be "active." They are obliged to consider the forms a just society should take, and ways to achieve them. Again, in the silence, self-control, and patience required by the tactics of passive resistance, they find an excellent school in the "passive" strength of religion. The intellectual resources from which such a transformation might grow are now latent on our campuses. They are carefully neglected.

Meanwhile, the student on the secular campus works out his religion for himself. Often his previous religious background will have been uncritical, informal, and unsophisticated; he may be the first member of his family pursuing a university education. His grasp of religious concepts like faith, hope, love may well be far less precise and intellectually defensible than it ought to be; his university career will offer him very little formal help in clarifying and criticizing them. It is possible that college life may be for him, then, a period of searing but private examination. For a time at least he may stop going to church or synagogue, and believe himself atheist or agnostic. But the chances are—in most schools and among most students—no such honest and fruitful personal critiques will occur, at least of any lasting depth. Where they do seem to occur, experienced religious men are pleased. "It's a more thoughtful kind of religion," seems to be the consensus of chaplains near Harvard. "It's better than merely going to church out of habit. They may be missing church services and undergoing changes now; but they'll be back when they return to their local communities and all the better for it."

But will they be? The fact seems to be that even among the more searching students, religion follows the pattern of their other personal convictions. The pattern of conformity they are taught in college, by which they systematically separate their inner convictions from the "objective" work of the classroom, will simply be continued in their business affairs, legal practice, or work of whatever kind in later life. A civilization pervaded by the laws and spirit of technology—on which profit and life itself are based— is a civilization prone to expediency and nonmoral, nonpersonal considerations. The vice of academicians is to become intellectual technologists; this vice prevails. The consequent bourgeois life of the American university becomes with hardly a hitch the middle-class life of the organization man and the suburbanite. The pretense of non-conformity and intellectual liberty on campus is seldom tested by real and fundamental disagreement; for such disagreement is usually "subjective" and not amenable to the kind of debate the university tacitly approves. "Liberals" and "conservatives" in politics, for example, seldom touch the basic issues separating them; they both try to argue in terms of "facts"; but why they are committed, each in his separate way, to different ideals, and what precisely these ideals are and whence they are derived—this kind of discussion does not suit the pragmatic and "objective" temper of present intellectual life. It is too intangible, dialectical, personal, however lethal in its effect upon action.

One might have hoped that the religiously committed private schools in America might have made by now some major contribution to American intellectual life. In part, they have been too concerned with putting up buildings, with more or less ghettolike defensiveness, and with hesitating between secular standards and their own long-ago tradition. In part, general American intellectual life rules out of professional discussion the very commitment which the religious schools primarily exist to foster. In any case, the potential strength of the religious school now goes almost for nought.

One might have hoped that religious men within the secular colleges might by their understanding and their leadership have restored to American universities a chance for a living and critical experience of religion. It is true that the Danforth Foundation, the National Council for Religion in Higher Education, and other groups are trying to favor the presence in our universities of talented religious men. But the strident tones of Fathers Feeney and Halton, and of William F. Buckley, Jr.'s essays and talks have sometimes soured the air. And for decades there have been too few men at once intellectual and religious and wise on the campuses. Vast empty spaces seem to surround the Niebuhrs and the Tillichs. The churches are filled with worshipers but intelligence has fled from the ranks of religion. Who or what can bring it back?

What, then, is the place of God in our colleges? The basic human experiences that remind man that he is not a machine, and not merely a temporary cog in a technological civilization, are not fostered within the university. God is as irrelevant in the universities as in business organizations; but so are love, death, personal destiny. Religion can thrive only in a personal universe; religious faith, hope, and love are personal responses to a personal God. But how can the immense question of a personal God even be posed and made relevant when fundamental questions about the meaning and limits of personal experience are evaded?

"God is dead. . . .What are these churches if they are not the tombs and sepulchers of God?" Nietzsche asked. But much of Western humanism is dead too. Men do not wander under the silent stars, listen to the wind, learn to know themselves, question, "Where am I going? Why am

I here?" They leave aside the mysteries of contingency and transitoriness, for the certainties of research, production, consumption. So that it is nearly possible to say: "Man is dead. . . . What are these buildings, these tunnels, these roads, if they are not the tombs and sepulchers of man?"

God, if there is a God, is not dead. He will come back to the colleges, when man comes back.

9 LAND WITHOUT LITURGY

Perhaps the best way to make clear how far America has become a land of technicians, where few are favored in their efforts to become persons, is to turn to the testimony of our literature. American religion has become so intertwined with the prejudices and narrownesses of American culture —when it has not itself favored them—that one of the recurrent themes of our national literature is the rebellion from religion. Theodore Dreiser in *An American Tragedy*, Sherwood Anderson in *Winesburg, Ohio*, Robert Penn Warren in *All the King's Men*, John Marquand in *The Late George Apley*, John Steinbeck in *The Grapes of Wrath*, Sinclair Lewis in *Elmer Gantry*, James T. Farrell in *Studs Lonigan*, Eugene O'Neill in *Long Day's Journey into Night* give no flattering picture of the role of religion in American consciousness. In *Huckleberry Finn*, a man died from a Bible being placed on his chest. Henry James was able to write a whole cycle of books with hardly a trace of religious emotion. As the years have gone on, it has been harder and harder for Americans to understand religion, except as a social tradition. Archibald MacLeish's attempt to create a believable God in *J.B.* not only failed in itself; the effort did not awaken much sympathy or comprehension in audiences or reviewers.

On the other hand, J. D. Salinger has book by book been finding his own way into the philosophy of the person. We have already alluded to the conversation between Franny and her date Lane in *Franny and Zooey*. Again in the story "Teddy" in *Nine Stories*, Salinger turns to the difference between technical and personal education. He presents a precocious ten-year-old who is talking, aboard ship in mid-Atlantic, to an Ivy League teacher of education:

> "You're just being logical," Teddy said to him impassively.
>
> "I'm just being what?" Nicholson asked, with a little excess of politeness.
>
> "Logical. You're just giving me a regular, intelligent answer," Teddy said. "I was trying to help you. You asked how I get out of the finite dimensions when I feel like it. I certainly don't use logic when I do it. Logic's the first thing you have to get rid of."
>
> Nicholson removed a flake of tobacco from his tongue with his fingers.
>
> "You know Adam?" Teddy asked him. . . . "You know what was in that apple? Logic. Logic and intellectual stuff. That was all that was in it. So—this is my point—what you have to do is vomit it up if you want to see things as they really are. I mean if you vomit it up, then you won't have any more trouble with blocks of wood and stuff. You won't see everything stopping off all the time. And you'll know what your arm really is, if you're interested. Do you know what I mean? Do you follow me?"
>
> "I follow you," Nicholson said, rather shortly.
>
> "The trouble is," Teddy said, "most people don't want to see things the way they are. . . ."

The tradition in which Salinger is standing is that of the Pascal of the first pages of the *Pensées*, and Dostoevsky and Camus on the "geometrical mind." This tradition accuses us of having committed a tragic epistemological mistake, of using knowledge to predict and to control things, even our own behavior, of treating even ourselves as things rather than as persons. However, Teddy misleadingly speaks of "logic" when he means a rationalistic point of view or a verbal way of looking at things. It is not the connection between premises and conclusions he is impugning; it is a technical attitude that takes the world as so many things to be looked at, studied, controlled.

John Updike is likewise in this tradition, less romantically than Salinger; he does not turn to the East for his insights, as Salinger appears to do. Yet Updike is often writing about man's search for personal immortality. He sometimes takes Protestant Christianity with ruthless seriousness. He is willing to try to understand life in American small towns and suburbs as it is now lived; he is not a prophet of dangerous living, nor a preacher of meaninglessness. He regularly refuses the values, the starting points, of the secular reformer. He does not take the lead in the causes the critics like to support; he sometimes takes a direction they fail to see.

To illustrate these points at length, I would like to invite close attention to the four-part story with which Updike closes *Pigeon Feathers*: "Packed Dirt, Churchgoing, A Dying Cat, A Traded Car." This story, I believe, is central to his work, and touches on nearly all his themes. It is as far in one direction as he has gone. It is one of the most perfectly worked pieces of prose in the English language, perhaps even overworked, too elaborate. Through its four sections, the story ascends in a complex spiral. Updike begins with images of a neighborhood path being destroyed by machines, and reflects on the interaction of men, machines, and nature; he next finds images for a contemplative view of the world; he confronts death; and last of all he confronts evil and finds an image for immortality. He seems to be struggling to find images, like Salinger in a more precious way, for that deep, serene, perennial way of looking at life which the secular, active West has lost.

"We in America need ceremonies, is I suppose, sailor, the point of what I have written;" so Updike concludes the present montage. Why do we in America need ceremonies? This is what Updike must show us. The first reason he suggests is that ceremonies are necessary, because through them we become human. But the second reason thrusts more sharply home: it is so that we will be able even to conceive what immortality is like, and therefore what we are like.

"Packed Dirt" concludes a cycle of stories. The title story, "Pigeon Feathers," catches the same hero, David Kern, in his more religious, small-town youth. Young David asks the minister at Sunday School (an experience like that of Philip Roth in "The Conversion of the Jews") "Where will Heaven be?" The minister replied in a forgiving tone: "David, you might think of Heaven this way: as the way the good that Abraham Lincoln did lives after him."

David is appalled. That means nothing. He is disgusted at this betrayal of Christianity, this ignorance compounded with a lie. His pseudo-religious mother tries to comfort him, and ensnares herself in worse ignorance, worse lies, worse sentiment.

" 'Mother, good grief. Don't you see'—he rasped away the roughness in his throat—'if when we die there's nothing, all your sun and fields and what not are all, ah, *horror?* It's just an ocean of horror.' " Young David "needed to begin to build his fortress against death. They none of them believed. He was alone. . . . All those sexy, perfumed people, wisecracking, chewing gum, all of them doomed to die, and none of them noticing," he alone recognizing that "we cannot, *cannot*, submit to death."

Now since Freud at least, it would be fashionable to think that something must be wrong with David: after all, people *don't* live forever and there's no need even for them to want to (his religious mother thinks he's greedy). But the young David Kern concludes his contemplation of the pigeons he has shot "robed in this certainty: that the God who had lavished such craft upon these worthless birds would not destroy His whole creation by refusing to let David live forever."

"Packed Dirt" opens with David Kern admitting that he is always "reassured, nostalgically pleased, even, as a member of my animal species made proud" by the sight of bare earth made firm by the passage of human feet. He is reassured, and that is the passive fruit of ceremony. He is made proud, for ceremony is an active victory won by his animal species.

Patches of packed dirt abound "in small towns"—not so

much in cities. They are "unconsciously humanized intervals of clay," made by the quiet interaction of men with the earth. They remind him of his childhood, "when one communes with dirt down among the legs, as it were, of abiding fatherly presences. The earth is our playmate then, and the call to supper has a piercingly sweet eschatological ring." To become as a little child is to treat the earth as a playmate, unself-consciously commune with things, be aware of a fatherly presence, know that the piercingly sweet call of death bids one home.

But machines enter the neighborhood to make way for cars, making "our rooms shake with the curses of their labor." The littlest Kern, not yet two, is frightened by the gnawing, mashing machines. By the next morning, however, the children—children, mostly, make paths—had treaded a path up the cliff left by the machines. This "modest work of human erosion" is one of those things which make Kern proud. It is a ceremony which seems precious to him, "not only because it recalled" his own childhood, but above all because "it had been achieved accidentally, and had about it that repose of grace that is beyond willing."

The children are at home with nature, but we "in America have from the beginning been cleaving and baring the earth, attacking, reforming the enormity of nature we were given, which we took to be hostile." The theme of American history has been: Conquer this continent; exalt man over nature. But now Updike estimates our triumph: "We have explored, on behalf of all mankind, this paradox: the more matter is outwardly mastered, the more it overwhelms us in our hearts." The scientific attitude is not the attitude of men, but of artisans. For men the world is not so much an enemy as a playmate, and if the war is "incapable of ceasing," it is, at least, "good to know that now there are enough of us to exert a counter-force"—enough to favor man over artisan.

"Churchgoing" begins just where "Packed Dirt" leaves off: it takes churchgoing "purely as a human recreation." From the human point of view alone, whether one chooses "to listen, or not listen, as a poorly paid but resplendently robed man strives to console us with scraps of ancient epistles and halting accounts, hopelessly compromised by words," churchgoing gives us a chance to be ourselves, to observe, to think. It is "the most available democratic experience," where, as at the polls, we are "actually given our supposed value, the soul-unit of one, with its noumenal arithmetic of equality: one equals one equals one." Sitting and standing in unison, we "sing and recite creeds and petitions that are like paths worn smooth in the raw terrain of our hearts." But even to describe churchgoing, Kern admits, is to corrupt it: it sounds much too preachy and self-conscious.

As a child, David Kern felt "nothing in church but boredom and an oppressive futility." Only at fifteen did he feel "a pleasant emotion in church," when on raw March nights during Lent he went in the family Chevrolet to usher with his father, while "the wind howled a nihilistic counterpoint beyond the black windows," and the "minority flock furtively gathered within the hostile enormity of a dying, sobbing empire." His restless father thought of church "as something he helped run," anxious for the moment to pass the plate. Young David felt like an initiate, smug, condescending, as he gallantly lowered the felt plate toward each pew of "The Others," and began to know the dangers of even the lowly honor of being usher.

He recalls, from later in his life, the "Second Century quality" of churches in the Village: "In Manhattan, Christianity is so feeble its future seems before it. . . . The expectantly hushed shelter of the church is like a spot worn bare by a softball game. . . . The presence of the city beats like wind at the glowing windows." He hurries home afterward "to assume the disguise" of a nonchurchgoer. He alternates churches, so as not to become among the known, who can look condescendingly on "The Others." "We are the others. It is of the essence to be a stranger in church." For though community is crucial, so likewise is personality uncluttered and naked in the sight of God.

On an island in the Caribbean, Kern attends a church in which he stands white among the dark natives. "For windows the church possessed tall arched apertures filled not with stained glass but with air and outward vision," and outside little girls were playing on "the packed dirt around the church." Yet in this moving setting, the "service was fatiguingly long," and natives who could hardly speak English were led through "exhaustive petitionary prayers (for the Queen, the Prime Minister, Parliament) and many eight-versed hymns sung with a penetrating, lingering joy. . . . Musical stress, the British accent, and Negro elision worked upon the words a triple harmony of distortion."

The church ceremony seems such a betrayal: Kern loses his place in the hymn—"without a visual key I was lost"— and, bored, turns from the restless deacons slipping in and out of the windows, toward "the earth's wide circle round." "The Caribbean seemed a steeply tilted blue plane to which the few fishing boats in the bay below had been attached like magnetized toys." The churches do not seem to understand symbol and ceremony any longer. They are as technological and dry as the cities of cement. They do not relate us to the earth. Updike concludes this section, too, with a philosopher: "God made the world, Aquinas says, in play." The Caribbean speaks with more eloquence than the church.

The third section, "A Dying Cat," begins with a brief meditation on the ambiguity of matter, but twists the spiral of the story upward from inanimate nature to the question of life and death: "Matter has its radiance and its darkness; it lifts and it buries. Things compete; a life demands a life."

From an island in the Caribbean, the scene shifts to "another English island," England itself, where on a lonely road late at night David Kern encounters something frightening which he does not then understand. America is somehow stifling for the religious man; we "receive our supernatural mail on foreign soil," and on the present incident the "signature" is "decisive but illegible." For six years Kern was unable to talk to his wife about it. Yet in itself the incident could have been innocuous: while his wife lies "swathed in white, ready for nothing so much as a graduation ceremony" in anticipation of childbirth, Kern comes upon a dying cat. It seemed to be, in the shadows, "about the size of a baby;" and of course it is as the cat dies that, that night, his perfect daughter is born.

Kern is determined not to let the cat die without ceremony. He laid her—he "felt it was female"—behind the hedge, and went back to his car to write a note to leave with her. Palm and three of the fingers of his glove are dyed a sacramental "wine-brown." The cat suffered his return stiffly: "It suggested I was making too much fuss, and seemed to say to me, *Run on home.*" He went back home, read from Chesterton's *The Everlasting Man*, prayed for his wife, and finally fell asleep.

The fourth and last section, "A Traded Car," is too long to follow in detail; as in the earlier parts, nearly every prominent word and surely every incident sends echoes forward and backward through the story. It opens: "When we returned from England, we bought a car." Before the paragraph is out, we are led to see that the car, if anything in America, is going to have to bear the symbolism that might help us understand ourselves. "Not only sand and candy wrappers accumulate in a car's interior, but heroisms and instants of communion. We in America make love in our cars, and listen to ball games, and plot our wooing of the dollar: small wonder the landscape is sacrificed to these dreaming vehicles of our ideal and onrushing manhood."

The ugly bulldozers push aside our paths to make room for highways; losing the symbols of nature, we gain the car. Kern and his wife treat their new '55 Ford as if it were a "broad blue baby," and it is not until their baby daughter born in England is nearly six that Kern can bring himself to trade it in. However, before relinquishing it to Detroit (who will "devour her child"), Kern has a last crucial adventure in the Ford.

At a dance with a woman not his wife, Kern falls sickeningly in love. The sweet desire leads to no more than her stroking his erect thumbs, but Kern's Sunday school conscience tells him that "to lust after a woman in thought is the same as committing adultery."

Unable to distinguish between automatic attraction and interior consent, Kern lies awake that night in terror. "To feel a sin was to commit it; to touch the brink was to be on the bottom of the chasm." But the real terror was that the "universe that so easily permitted me to commit adultery became . . . a universe that would easily permit me to die. The enormities of cosmic space, the maddening distension of time, history's forgotten slaughters, the child smothered in the dumped icebox, the recent breakdown of the molecular life-spiral, the proven physiological roots of the mind, the presence in our midst of idiots, Eichmanns, animals, and bacteria—all this evidence piled on, and I seemed already eternally forgotten . . . I prayed . . . prayed, prayed for a sign, any glimmer at all. . . . Each second my agony went unanswered justified it more certainly: the God who permitted me this fear was unworthy of existence."

Intensely moved, Kern awakens his wife to tell her he is frightened; pragmatically, a little bored, she gives him the Stoic answer; he falls asleep as on the night of that other encounter with death. A phone call the next day tells him his father is dying. "Instantly I was relieved. The weight on me rolled away. All day death had been advancing under cover and now it had struck, declared its position."

A visit to church that night, and next day he begins his drive to Pennsylvania. "*Run on home.*" He picks up a hitchhiking sailor, one of those "docile Titans—guileless, competent, mildly earnest—that we have fattened, an ocean removed from the slimming Latin passions and Nordic anxieties of Europe."

The writer, Kern, and the nameless sailor have little to talk about; yet their relationship is not at all that of brilliant isolated artist and the beautiful blond beast that Thomas Mann describes in the stories of the *Death in Venice* cycle. Updike is not after the Platonic distinction in types of men, the elite and the herd; he is after the incomprehension, the shallowness, the easy adjustment, the lack of life in our scientized environment, our "abundance of milk and honey, vitamins and protein." It sometimes seems that natural wealth, science, and pragmatic adjustment are enough; and in this environment, how can one hear of God or immortality?

A little later, the sailor gone, Kern stops at a Howard

Johnson's in the Mennonite country; the waitresses remind him of an earlier time, of "that Pennsylvania knowingness—of knowing, that is, that the truth is good." At home, his mother pours him a glass of wine: "Wine had a ceremonial significance in our family; we drank it seldom." His mother tells him his father has "lost his faith." "He never was much of one for faith," she adds. "He was strictly a works man."

The next day, mother and son visit the family doctor; Kern has time to reminisce about the order, delight, and hope of childhood. Knowing his own faith gone, too, he follows his mother into the hospital. Leading him, she is already exercising the responsibilities of widowhood.

In the ensuing conversation with the older Kern, David finds his father talking mostly of how he'll miss his car. Just as David begins to feel the coming separation with his father (and cannot speak of it for "there were no words, no form of words available in our tradition"), and as his mother is already weeping, a girl from the Lutheran Home Missions comes to visit, notebook in hand. Young Kern is afraid she'll be made fun of; far from it, the older Kern tells her after a warm conversation, "You're a wonderful woman to be doing what you're doing." The woman leaves "transformed into just that. As a star shines in our heaven though it has vanished from the universe, so my father continued to shed faith upon others." A cat's dying balanced a baby's birth: a law of continuity, a kind of permanence.

For the first time, David realizes that when he says "home" he means "a far place, where I had a wife and children." His father is not going to die just yet and, though it comes as a disappointment to the bedridden man, David tell him he must return home. In an instant during which his face was blank, the older Kern "was swallowing the realization that he was no longer the center of even his son's universe." As David is about to drive north, his mother reminds him of the night he was born, when his father drove north from Wheeling: "the story of his all-night ride was the first myth in which I was a character."

Driving home in the sunset, Kern enters a new myth. Pennsylvania again reminds him of repose, of "the certainty that the truth is good." "It seemed to me for this sunset hour that the world is our bride, given us to love, and the terror and joy of the marriage is that we bring to it a nature not our bride's." But if the world is not of our nature, what shall we find to symbolize for us what our nature is like?

Like Kern's nighttime fall through an empty universe, the car ride begins to seem "meaninglessly coquettish," then "maddeningly obstinate," then "frighteningly empty." A "stellar infinity of explosive sparks" is needed to drive the effortlessly moving car, and these pass into his body. He stops for coffee and "the hallucinatory comfort of human faces"; the music on the radio obliterated time; it "began to seem a miracle that the car could gather speed" from his numb foot.

Gradually, the car becomes David Kern's soul, as little by little he leaves his body. "We climbed through a space fretted by scattered brilliance and bathed in a monotonous wind. I had been driving forever; furniture, earth, churches, women, were all things I had innocently dreamed. And through those aeons my car, beginning as a mechanical spiral of molecules, evolved into something soft and organic and consciously brave. I lost, first, heart, then head, and finally any sense of my body. In the last hour of the trip I ceased to care or feel or in any real sense see, but the car, though its soul the driver had died, maintained steady forward motion, and completed the endless journey safely."

Out of flux, Updike fashions a symbol of permanence, of spirit, in which we might at last be able even to understand immortality. But the very car which furnishes him this symbol, that six-year-old Ford, is soon to be traded in for a new one: "when he returned the car would be new, and the old one was gone, gone, utterly dissolved back into the mineral world from which it was conjured, dismissed without a blessing, a kiss, a testament, or any ceremony of farewell."

In a pragmatic, secular America, it is almost impossible for faith to take intelligent root, and men, though having ears, cannot hear; for there are almost no correlates in our experience for what the Word of God says. Even though he is so far limiting himself to his own experience, John Updike is beginning to make the experiences basic to religion intelligible in America, and to fashion symbols whereby man can understand many things about himself which, especially in America, he has forgotten. It is not surprising if the critics see only the dazzling words, and do not grasp what they mean. "We in America need ceremonies," is, I suppose, the point of a great many of the words he has written.

Where the imagination is starved for liturgy, intelligence can only be technical or functional. The problem of the new generation is to create a fuller, American humanism—lest the spiritual life of secular America and of Catholic America wither and die: seed cannot take root on rocks. But this task immediately involves practical—and theoretical—difficulties in American schools.

10 THE IDEA OF DISSENT

Two of these difficulties, especially, already trouble our generation: the related questions of parochial and public education. On the one hand, it has become clear that the goal of "every Catholic child in a Catholic school" is unattainable. Moreover, an increasing number of laymen, priests, and bishops are asking whether it is, even in principle, desirable. What are Catholic schools attempting to do? Do they succeed? Is there a better way? On the other hand, the fact remains that approximately one half of all Catholic students are in public, not Catholic, institutions. Catholics are beginning to give an increasing amount of attention, reflection, and energy to the public schools. These two questions, particularly the former, preoccupy us in this chapter; in the next two chapters we will concentrate on the public school and the secular university.

Closely related to the concept of the person which we have been at some pains to suggest is the idea of dissent. The idea of dissent is at the root of the controversy of our decade over federal aid to education. Dissent involves the workings of human understanding, and these workings in turn involve questions about the aims of education. The roots of a genuine humanism lie in epistemology: man is a knowing animal, and whatever a man takes knowing to be, that he takes man to be. An epistemological problem is at the roots of the political and social debate over education. For that reason, a study of the idea of dissent attacks the problem at the most fruitful level.

Dissent is a two-edged sword. It cuts both ways in the current debate. Dissent furnishes the basic argument for those who favor a multiple school system in America, with each system receiving proportionate aid from the state. On the other hand, dissent furnishes the basic argument for those who favor only a single, public school system, at least so far as state aid is concerned. The latter argue that the American Constitution has institutionalized dissent; thus, that there cannot be for Americans an official orthodoxy on the fundamental questions of life. But the exclusion of orthodoxy from the public schools has not ended there; we have gone on to exclude even consideration of fundamental questions from the public schools. In a curious reversal of roles, those who claim to represent the tradition of dissent that stems from the Enlightenment are often arguing for a unified, homogeneous, nondivisive school system; while those who more usually claim to represent unity and docility are often arguing for a dissenting, multiple school system.

Initially, it is helpful to recall the sociological reasons for this reversal of roles. In the first place, until the immigration laws of 1924 closed off the main influx of new peoples to our land, and until those millions who came before that date became "acculturated," the main task of American education was to instruct its new peoples in American traditions, to unify them, to form of them one people. There was always, of course, a danger in this concept of unifying, even when it is called "democratizing." But that danger is heightened now that the shut-off date of the great immigration which gave it justification is some thirty-five years past. American liberals, who are so much opposed elsewhere to the forces of homogenization and standardization in our society, have not revised their concept of the task of the public schools as the threat from immigration has subsided. How could so many American intellectuals continue to approve a homogenizing school system which has a distinct world view?

To many American liberals, the ultimate questions of religious belief or unbelief are not intellectual questions, not questions for school; they are matters of private concern. Moreover, to those who do not believe in God, questions about ultimates are meaningless; an education that confines itself to arts, sciences and technics is perfectly adequate to their world view. It does not occur to such men—for their view seems perfectly natural to them—that the "godless" education of which they approve is exactly the one which fails to meet the world view of other American citizens. In the view of many nonbelievers, dissenting education is a luxury; if you want it, you must pay for it.

The sociopolitical background of the various religious groups in America further explains this reversal of roles. Roman Catholics are, as a group, almost alone in being so concerned about education as to desire to dissent from the world view that rules education in the public schools, and thus to build their own system. Protestants early benefited by the Protestant orientation of the public schools; more lately, many of them have become so afraid of what they refer to as "Catholic power" that they do not seem to worry about the world view of the public schools. (Unfortunately, some Catholic ecclesiastics and laymen do use the communion of the faithful as a power bloc.) Furthermore, most Protestants have not the same drive toward making faith and intelligence, on their separate levels, work together upon every problem as Catholics do. They seem more easily able to separate their philosophy, art, economics and other "secular" concerns from their faith. They quite readily go along with nonbelievers on almost every earthly issue, holding their faith safely aside.

There is, however, a long tradition of Catholicism which finds it impossible to live, as it were, in two worlds; for this Catholic tradition, there is only one world. It is in this present world of philosophy, art, science, and politics that one comes to understand and to live one's faith; everything and every event has its religious aspect, nothing is merely secular or profane. And of course this integral world view does not find expression in the state schools. Among American Jews, finally, there seems to be a resentment of the

Christian orientation of the public schools; and whether for religious reasons or for cultural reasons (since Jews remain Jews even when they no longer share religious belief), American Jews seem in the main to favor the increased secularization of the public schools and the homogenization of a single school system. The resurgence of the schools attached to the synagogues, however, indicates renewed Jewish concern about a dissenting form of education.

But when these considerations of the sociological background are set aside, we must still ask, what is dissent in education? The question of dissent is confused because we have witnessed in our culture in recent centuries an amusing struggle between the enlightened avant garde and the reluctant majority. Very often, obviously so in scientific questions, the avant garde has been proved in time to have been correct: but often too (for example, in the estimation which many American intellectuals of the twenties and thirties held for the Soviet experiment) time has not supported the avant garde. The avant garde generally thinks that every position it takes is anchored in science; and since in our time science has been systematically advancing beyond old frontiers, dissent has sometimes come to be taken, by the avant garde, as very nearly a value in itself: another sign of imminent advance. Correspondingly, dissent has often come to be taken by the "solid, respectable elements in society" as the sign of yet another bright and untried idea, if not of sheer restless indocility; those who dissent are those who simply cannot make the grade in life as it is. Dissent has come to have a sort of mythic value—a magazine, a prominent book can use the word as a title—and society can be divided as "liberal" or "conservative" depending (in part) on how individuals stand toward that myth.

In science and in daily living, however, it is neither dissent nor conformity that is crucial. In intellectual and moral matters, it doesn't matter whether one is standing alone or with the majority. What is crucial is an understanding of relevant facts, and the possession of evidence to support one's understanding. The aim of education, therefore, is neither dissent nor conformity. It is the furtherance of the drive to understand. At times, fidelity to understanding calls for dissent; at times, it calls for conformity. To be original does not suffice; one can be original and wrong. Nor does the support of others suffice. Understanding is the key factor in education; it is the root value upon which dissent draws; its unlimited goal is the justification for pluralism; it is the moderator between all factions, whose standards each faction must meet.

By understanding, I mean the familiar activity which everyone can experience in himself, the "I get it!," the insight which the intelligent experience often and easily, and the dull find difficult and rare. The advantage of using this activity rather than any other as the key factor in education is that it is eminently personal to each student, and that it involves every other activity of the person. It is eminently personal because only the individual can, at his own pace and in his own way, grasp the point. The teacher can lead him to all the information, teach him the right words, and how to manipulate the relevant concepts, but the teacher cannot make him understand. It is understanding that distinguishes education from indoctrination, and is the individual's strength against ideology and propaganda. Society can provide slogans, concepts, training programs, even machines; but it does not in this way ensure understanding. In education, the most society can do is provide an environment in which youth will be stimulated, not automatically to dissent or to conform, but to try to understand.

The second advantage to choosing understanding as the key notion of education is that understanding involves every other activity of the person. More than anything else in education, the student must come to understand himself. But understanding is a conscious, not a blind, activity; in understanding, a man draws on his memory, present experience, imaginative arrangement of all the data, and acquaintance with relevant concepts and techniques. None of these other activities substitutes for understanding. But in the moment of understanding, all of them are present. The difficulty is that rationalists in educational theory concern themselves chiefly with concepts and the techniques of handling them (definition, induction, deduction, etc.), and romantics attend chiefly to memory, experience, and imagination. But understanding needs all of these activities, the romantic and the rationalist both. In proportion as a student understands all the activities of which he is capable, and their role in understanding, he is in a position to use his understanding upon whatever problem confronts him.

The aim of education is to understand, and understanding is an activity requiring the whole person. Thus, a restriction upon those things to be studied needs careful justification. Such a restriction may be grounds for dissent from an education that is inadequate. It does not do to say, for example, that matters of ultimate concern are too difficult to study, or that men's positions upon them are pluralistic, and therefore lie outside the field of education. Realistic education cannot overlook the fact of the differences among men, the implications of these differences and the reasons for them.

There are four major positions vis-à-vis man's destiny taken up in America: Protestant, Catholic, Jewish, and nonbelieving humanist. The history of these groups is tangled and interrelated; the intellectual positions of each have points of contact and points of sharp disagreement; the attitudes of each toward man and society show marked differences, and some similarity. Children sitting side by side in the classroom cannot begin to understand how they are united to each other, and how they are different from each other, unless the various relationships between these groups are discussed. Again, if the holidays, Jewish and Christian, which impinge upon the school year pass without classroom discussion, education has a remoteness and abstraction from concrete reality which dodges the demands of understanding. The measure of education is man. For the aim of education is that man should understand himself. In our society, there are several positions on what man is, and no one in our society can understand himself unless he understands these positions and the one among them which he chooses as his own.

In America of the 1960's, we still do not trust each other; and we do not trust our public school teachers. As a result, we do not allow our teachers even to mention the issues of ultimate concern: is there a God? how is man related to Him? what is man? how should man order his activities? We do not even allow our teachers to dwell on how Protestants differ from Catholics, or why the Jewish children celebrate different holidays than the Christian children, or what the differences are, in world view and in social action, for those who believe in God and those who don't.

In the first place, our teachers—like ourselves—are colossally ignorant about these differences. In the second place, it is as difficult in these matters as in others for a teacher not to sway students by his or her persuasion; and we spontaneously feel that these matters are too important for such suasion. Yet it does seem a trifle silly that if these matters are so important we will not have them talked about at all. The fact is that we are distrustfully, almost bitterly, at variance with one another; and we refuse in our public schools to bring this fact out into the open, making our schools as pluralistic as our society is.

So long then as the American consensus is to allow the

public schools to hide from a full understanding of man in our society, there seems no choice but for those to whom ultimate concerns are important to dissent from the public schools and found schools of their own. Their dissent is based not only on a desire to pursue education according to their own world view, but also on a critique of the existing world view of the public schools. Through intellectual cowardice, abetted by memories of past bitterness, the public schools do not discuss the most profound issues of knowledge and life. The public schools are thereby bankrupting the deepest springs of Western culture; they have turned out by now more than a generation of Americans who have not discussed the ultimate questions about men, and their differences, in their formal education. Furthermore, there is no forum in the public schools so that those at least aware of the bankrupting might protest it; such ultimate considerations are simply excluded.

But the principle of dissent cuts both ways. If Catholics, for example, use the principle of dissent to demand equal status before the law for their own educational world view, and to justify their refusal—which, they argue, should not be penalized—to accept the world view of the public schools, then they must attend to the workings of that principle of dissent *within* their own school system. For the aim of education is understanding, not conformity; self-knowledge, not false docility; independence, not repetition. Catholic schools do not yet understand, or cherish, the principle of dissent. This is not to say that Catholic education has not progressed greatly since the Second World War: in physical plant, in resources, in deeper motivation and self-criticism. Catholic education has expanded to a larger circle of achievement. But within that circle of achievement, a new energy is building up to break out again for a new advance. A restlessness is apparent in many places; and it seems that that restlessness can best come to focus in an appreciation of the notion of dissent—not for dissent's sake, but insofar as dissent is based on understanding.

In nearly every parish in the land, there are now laymen better versed in their respective fields than their pastors: laymen skilled in the problems of investment, financing, building, psychology, sociology, education theory. Not until these laymen make their contributions to the establishment and policies of the parochial schools will these schools truly be theirs. At present, there exists no institutional form in which the layman can make a contribution; his knowledge and skills are hardly tapped; he sits passively by, asked only for money. It was even notable, in 1961, how often clerics, not the Catholic parents whose rightful task it was, spoke out on the political issue of aid to the Catholic schools. It ill becomes the clergy to speak in the name of Catholic parents, when these parents have the education and stature to speak for themselves; it ill becomes the clergy to direct Catholic education only by their own wisdom, when these parents have much wisdom of their own to share.

Many Catholic laymen do not approve of parochial

schools; many do not approve of sending their children to Catholic schools for their *entire* education; and many cherish the parochial schools very dearly—the voices of all these laymen should be heard. Within the schools, there is no reason why knowledgeable laymen should not be consulted about curricula, texts, and teachers, if the schools are to be theirs. Nor is there any reason why they should not voice their desires concerning uniforms and other policies.

On the part of students, too, there is a need for an appreciation of the value and techniques of dissent based upon understanding. The exaggerated respect with which Catholic students are taught to respond to nuns, brothers, or priests is an obstacle to frankness and person-to-person criticism. Exaggerated respect on the college level, particularly in girls' colleges, is especially disheartening; one wonders how there can be any maturity or health either for the student or for the religious involved. For education demands straightforward, plain human relationships; if students are to dissent from a nun or a priest, they have got to be able to tell the often ugly truth, without apology or overmuch courtesy. The main tragedy of American Catholic education is that it is excruciatingly difficult to be perfectly honest with nuns, priests, or overprotected students. Nothing is so easy as to scandalize American Catholics; new ideas, new approaches, new criticisms make them distinctly if not vocally uncomfortable. Catholic students need clear means of showing vigorous disagreement

—which will sometimes appear disrespectful, skeptical, frightening—to no matter whom.

The demands of the drive to understand which underlies healthy dissent are relentless and unyielding. In the current debate on the public and parochial schools these demands work in both directions. They ask the proponents of the present public schools how they can afford to bury their heads, ostrichlike, rather than face the ultimate pluralism of our people, and the ultimate issues of Western civilization. They ask the proponents of the parochial schools how they can afford to stand on the principle of dissent to justify aid to parochial schools, without advancing in thorough appreciation of the principle of dissent within the parochial schools.

Perhaps the best that can be hoped in this educational debate of our generation is that each participant give full rein in himself to the demands of the drive to understand, revise his own educational theory accordingly, and thus come to meet with other men in pursuing the same drive. It is probably too much to ask of those who are not Catholic that they defend the Catholic dissent from the world view of the public schools and urge no penalty for such dissent. Just so, it is no doubt too much to hope that Catholics grow up in one short generation to full and creative stature, according to the yet unrealized possibilities of their own vision of man, by a new appreciation of dissent based upon understanding. Yet there is already evidence that both hopes are warranted. The theme of wise dissent is gaining momentum in Catholic schools and publications. Among non-Catholics—as we shall now see—support for the Catholic dissent from a single public school system is mounting. On the other hand, separate private systems are not a sufficient answer to our problems. The chief problem lies in the public schools.

11 Religion in the Public Schools

One of the most admirable qualities of the liberal mind is its openness to argument; among liberals, perhaps no virtue is so cherished. Every virtue has its flaws and is sometimes made precious by disuse; vis-à-vis Roman Catholics, the American liberal has sometimes been disdainful and unfair. But nowhere has his largeness of spirit been more in evidence than in the widespread acceptance of the most reasonable Catholic arguments for federal aid to parochial education. The change in the position of the New Republic from 1961 to 1963 was most remarkable. In the same period, Dean Griswold of Harvard, Robert Hutchins, and Walter Lippmann spoke out, each with his own accent, in favor of some form of aid to parochial schools. The ground on which these men generally chose to stand was that the good of the nation requires the education of all her youth; if fifteen percent of these youths are permitted to attend parochial schools, then the nation can not afford to give them an inferior education. But they also showed themselves aware of the question of free dissent; and Dean Griswold and the editors of the New Republic in particular took clear and vigorous exception to secular absolutism. Such absolutism thrusts an abstract principle, a metaphor at that, in the face of the concrete history of our land. Its "wall of separation between Church and State" is as unhistorical, as unpolitical, as the ideal thesis about the union of Church and State propounded by such authors as Ryan and Boland. The political philosophy of American democracy must be distorted, to be made to fit the views and methods of such absolutism or such idealism.

Nevertheless, most of the discussion, by Catholics and non-Catholics alike, has been directed at the question of church-related schools; this is not yet the heart of the argument. The crucial problem lies in the public schools. It may be granted that the parochial schools do not exist to separate Catholic children from secular culture, but to give them every secular advantage *together with* something the public schools do not give: education in religion. It may also be granted that the instruction in the parochial schools is so organized, or can without loss be made so, that it would meet the standards of the American public in most secular subjects. There are problems in literature and history, but not insoluble ones. Catholics, for example, may find more to respond to in a poet like Gerard Manley Hopkins or T. S. Eliot, than religiously neutral teachers may point out; so long as Catholic teachers do not slight the secular or the rebellious writers, such emphasis is pedagogically sound. Correspondingly, history textbooks in the public schools are sometimes years behind the best contemporary scholarship; their treatment of the Catholic period of Western history is sometimes insensitive and anachronistic. Much would be gained if Catholic textbook writers were to sit down with their secular counterparts to work out texts suitable for both public and parochial education.

But the American public needs desperately to be warned against the deadliness inherent in that form of educational compromise which avoids controversy. There is no greater cancer in American life than the fear of controversy. In a review in the *New Republic* (March 16, 1963), Paul Goodman warned that the American high school course is "more and more tightly standardized, scheduled, and graded. . . . Rival world views, whether folk, traditional, sectarian, or artistically and philosophically heretical, are less and less available; the exposure to the one world view is always more intense and swamping. . . . Suppose a young fellow happens to become disaffected from this 'reality.' He is not likely to know of other possibilities of philosophy, political dissent, religious faith, artistic tradition, free science. He is almost forced to withdraw into his own guts . . . to exploit the public style as a hipster for his private power." The effort to make parochial schools conform to public standards should not go so far that it destroys their distinctiveness.

Even if the parochial schools retain their special character, subject to public satisfaction and assisted by public funds for secular purposes, still, 85 percent of our children are in the public schools. They are the ones most endangered by the "swamping" Mr. Goodman describes. Catholic children in parochial schools are at least aware of an alternative: they can lose their faith. The fear which Americans have of offending one another—or of being offended—the fear of ideas not their own, creates a problem for the public schools more significant than the problem created by the presence of parochial schools. This is the problem of religion in the public schools, and this problem has hardly been touched.

The secular thinker, of course, does not think that religion has anything essential to contribute to education, because it has little to say about the good life. Religion seems to him an accident, an archaic residue from the Old World, like Swedishness or Irishness, which must pass away. "God," John Dewey said, "is the union of the ideal and the actual," in a connection in which he meant that religion consists in the realizing of justice and fellow feeling in the social and political order.

To the religious man, however, education is more than training in the skills, insights, and techniques of social and political action. It must also deal with man's destiny, his history, the identity of the individual, his hierarchy of goals, his motivations. In their professional disciplines, the religious and the secular thinker may be at one in their methods and their conclusions; on questions such as these others, they are no longer of the same spirit. If the public schools do not treat of such questions, on the grounds that they are divisive or are not amenable to scientific resolution, then from the religious point of view the public schools are favoring the secularist; for it is a moot point whether how to live the good life is a secular inquiry. As things are now, the student in the public school may officially be taught that it is "undemocratic" to treat the Negro unfairly; but he may not be taught that the Negro stands equal with him in the sight of God, and is in fact more beloved because he suffers more.

It is of little avail for a freshman to come to Purdue or UCLA with religious ideas that have had no development since Calvin, and were learned by rote at home or at church. He needs to know what he means when he says "God." He needs to know by what criteria God judges human action and how eternity and time, religion and secular concerns, are related. He needs to decide to what religious tradition or authority he can most confidently turn for sophistication, criticism, and stimulation of his own inquiries. He needs to weigh the impact of history, the discoveries of science, and the fashions of philosophy upon the content of his beliefs. He is responsible for the intellectual creativity of religion in his time, as his forebears were in theirs. He is the agent by which religion will, or will not, intellectually appropriate the lessons of his culture, and thus continue the dialogue between God and His people which advances through history.

Now it is unrealistic to think that the intellectual task awaiting the religious man can be done entirely outside his schooling, after hours, at Sunday School, in the church basement. (Both John Updike and Philip Roth give us images of that.) If religion is intellectually bankrupt in America, with little understanding or restless ferment or even consistency, surely it is because of the abysmal state of religious education. It cannot be otherwise when the Sunday School is so far from the business offices, when the public school limits religion to irrelevance, when the petty quarrels among religious peoples prevent them from seeing the magnitude of their common educational task. America does not benefit by millions of church-goers not seeming to see the relevance of the Gospels or biblical history to the intellectual and social struggles of our time. It does no good for a religious people to strain the gnat of a ruling against prayer before classes, only to swallow the camel of a nonintellectual religion.

Nor are separate religious schools the solution. The parochial school system is gradually giving Roman Catholics the most highly educated laity in the Church's history; but for various reasons, especially the lack of intellectual tradition in most Catholic families, the expedient of a separate school system is not producing the results the nation might hope of it. Upon graduation, students from Catholic schools are scarcely distinguishable from their companions from the public schools. The Catholics overload their teaching nuns and make money-raisers and school-builders of their priests, in the impossible hope of putting "every Catholic child in a Catholic school," only to find that preoccupation with money and administration has caused them to lose touch with the Gospels, and that their children are often as religiously unmotivated and uncritical as the rest.

Religion in America—intellectually weak, academically irrelevant, and often publicly hypocritical—will not be revivified until it is effectively present in the public schools. The attempt in these schools to stay neutral on ultimate questions means in practice that ultimate questions are not raised; and those for whom secular purposes, values, and motivations are finally meaningless receive no help in formulating other views of life than the secular view. It is no excuse to say that such help would be divisive; we live in a pluralistic country. It is no excuse to say that such help is not essential; that is already to take the secular view.

It may, however, be an excuse to ask: Who would teach these courses in questions of belief? How could interparty suspicions and fears be overcome? Would Catholics entrust their children to explanations given by an atheist? Would the children of atheists be affronted by the teaching of a Seventh Day Adventist? The difficulties are formidable; even their formulation has yet to be attempted. But the alternative is to surrender this nation to a secular vision of life, which, in the judgment of many of us, would be a misfortune.

What beginnings can be made toward a solution? In these days of ecumenical enthusiasm and exchange, it may at last be possible for Protestant, Catholic, Jewish, and secular scholars to sit down and prepare pilot textbooks explaining conjointly the history and purposes of their various world views. Geddes MacGregor's *Introduction to Religious Philosophy* is one book, among others, that may sugggest a neutral way to put the questions. Ministers, priests, rabbis, and secular thinkers might be drawn into the program, either in the teachers colleges or in the public schools themselves; but as scholars, not as preachers. Who knows? In the sparks and questionings that might fly, perhaps American education would be at its liveliest in decades, with the whole populace drawn into the discussions. It would begin to matter what one thought. Religious commitment, of course, must be left to the individual's private conscience, to his personal advisers and confidants, to the churches. But the notions, the alternatives, and the presuppositions and the reasons for them, can be taught in the public school.

But isn't religion "caught, not taught?" Catholic students often complain that their religion courses are the dullest and least satisfactory in the curriculum; why should we carry this dullness into the public school? Even courses on "world religions" in nonsectarian prep schools and universities are notoriously innocuous and boring. Religious concepts need to be taught, for they do not merely "happen," and they are often difficult and upsetting; but *how* should they be taught? I suggest that the teaching of religion in the parochial school and the sectarian class is dull because it is one-sided; it does not answer the questions of life. Children are shown one path to insight, one set of concepts, whereas the human mind is many-sided. Roman Catholic children, for example, would be better *Catholics* if they learned their faith in the light of alternatives. At each age level there are appropriate methods for presenting alternatives, without demanding of the child powers of discrimination beyond his years, or raising him as an abiding agnostic. Clearly teenagers have questions which a one-sided education cannot answer; it is no accident that apostasies from the traditional faiths which are confirmed in college have usually been well-advanced in high school.

The teaching of religion in the public schools would necessarily avoid the one-sidedness of parochial education. But everything depends on how searching the teaching is. If the teacher tries to be noncontroversial, to challenge no one, to upset no one, it would be better for him not to teach religion. Here Socrates is correct: religious notions are among those which cannot be learned except through inner confusion, unsettling questions, and progressive change of personal attitudes and beliefs. There are, consequently, two general criteria for the realistic teaching of religion in an open, public forum like the public schools: (1) the presentation of the alternatives must be *fair*; adult representatives of each group must have an opportunity to formulate the teaching, whether in the textbooks or in the classroom; (2) the presentation must be *realistic, applied, concrete*. Each religious view has its advantages and disadvantages when confronted with certain political, social, or personal facts. The student must be led to see that if he chooses one alternative he must have reasons strong enough to counterbalance the disadvantages pointed out by textbooks, teachers, and classmates; and he must have help in formulating these reasons.

I do not see how such teaching can fail to be disturbing, controversial, and beneficial. The good will requisite to the preparation of textbooks and teachers, and the supplanting of present mutual suspicion by mutual trust, will be hard to summon up, but the time seems ripe and, in any case, argument among free men is democracy's *raison d'être*. It is only in the public schools that religion can become relevant to the actual notions of Americans about the goals of this nation and the characteristics of the good life for the community and the person. The split between religion and public education is one reason for the present coexistence among our people and their leaders of the platitudinous and the amoral. There has been so much silence for so long that the task of presenting religion in the public schools is of forbidding proportions; the cure for that is hard work now.

Next to the public schools, the secular universities are the greatest spiritual force in American culture. But from the point of view of the Western tradition on the human person, not all is well on the secular campus. There are more than enough "blond beasts" in open collars and moccasins, whose world is bounded by the music they hear, the magazines they read, the sporting rites at which they are devotés, the necking parties and dances they plan to attend. There are many who appear to live without consciousness of what it is to be themselves, who drift, who are apathetic, and bored. There are others who are still capable of enthusiasm for the race to "success"; thankfully, their numbers appear to be dwindling as they observe the lives of the preceding generation. Yet at the best of the secular schools—Swarthmore, Yale, Harvard, Dartmouth and others—it still appears possible to get the best traditionally personalistic education available in our land. Without the rhetoric about "synthesis" so prominent in brochures about Catholic colleges, without any controlled effort at unity or wholeness, the very creativity and diversity of the free secular environment seems to favor the development of self-critical, integrated persons. If many of these persons have not integrated religious experience and insights into the rest of their life, if they do not seem to have a personalistic vocabulary in which to express their own best achievements, if as we have seen their gravest temptation is toward treating human intelligence as only technical, these are deficiencies in contemporary secular education. Still, the secular campus is the most exciting home for the human spirit in our time.

Thus, if aimed only at Catholic colleges, the question "Where are the Catholic intellectuals?" is missing a large part of the target. For there are at present some 500,000 Catholic students on secular campuses, and some 300,000 on Catholic campuses. This proportion seems to mean that in the near future five eighths of the most highly placed Catholics in American cultural life will be graduates of secular colleges. The question we have not been asking, then, is: Where are the Catholic intellectuals from secular campuses? What happens to the promising young Catholics who go to secular colleges and graduate schools? And how is the American Church helping them?

It is almost impossible to account for the incredibly meager aid which the American Church is giving her half-million sons and daughters on secular campuses. It is almost as if they simply weren't there. The Catholic Almanac for 1962, for example, devotes a number of pages to a complete statistical study, state by state, of the entire Catholic school system. It has not a single word about the half-million

Catholics at secular colleges, not to mention the more than 3.3 million (1959) in public elementary or high schools. The Almanac does have a short note, not under "Education" but under "Youth," on the Newman clubs: it notes that the 546 nationally affiliated clubs have 50,000 members. (It notes also that there are another 325 unaffiliated clubs, membership not given.)

In his recent paperback, *Catholics on Campus*, William J. Whalen affirms that one out of five Catholics on campus joins the Catholic clubs. Thus four out of five, some 400,000 Catholic students—*one third more again than those in all Catholic colleges together*—have no contact with the Church on campus. Furthermore, for these half-million students, Whalen counts only 140 full-time chaplains in the Newman clubs. Some of these full-time chaplains divide their time between four or five campuses. Again, comparing the Almanac's 871 Catholic clubs to the Merriam-Webster list of colleges in the United States, it is plain that there are many hundreds of secular campuses not known to have a Catholic club or chaplain at all.

The percentage of Catholic students on secular campuses varies from two per cent to sixty-seven, and averages fifteen. The percentage of Catholic faculty members lags very far behind, very often at two per cent or less. This means that in some departments, and sometimes in entire schools, a Catholic of intellectual standing is unknown. The Newman club chaplain, if there is one, often lacks university experience in his own past. The campus tradition, therefore, is hardly touched by a Catholic intellectual tradition. More-over, even in his pastoral role—and since the source of Catholic life is the liturgy, this emphasis seems fitting—the chaplain is overwhelmed by the numbers he faces, and so again the campus is hardly touched.

When the lone chaplain on a huge secular campus, whose Catholics number more than those in the neighboring Catholic college, thinks of the countless students who never come to him, he must look with longing at the band of priests on the Catholic campus. New York University, with ten thousand Catholics, is "the largest Catholic campus in the world." What could its chaplain do with the eighty-nine priests and brothers who care for six thousand students at Notre Dame, or the seventy Jesuits allotted to the twelve hundred boys at Holy Cross?

It is obvious that educated Catholics will not only be the influential Catholics of the future, but also the ones most likely to communicate their advantages to others. Hence, it is difficult to see why the American Church does not give at least as much attention to her students, wherever they are, as to her parishes. It is difficult to see why she does not invest far more care in them. It is also difficult to see why priests are not assigned in a more fruitful balance between Catholic and secular campuses. Even a small shift in the present proportion might be healthy for both groups. (More administrative tasks could, for example, be opened to laymen in Catholic colleges, and more pastoral work could fall to the lot of priests.)

As it is, most Catholics on a secular campus have no contact with the Church. What help do they receive when they attend the nearest parish? It is sad to report that they are often harmed. Let us take a fictitious and extreme example, but one that might be found occasionally in any region of the country. A local pastor is quite unsympathetic to the world outside Catholicism. He has not experienced a secular education, has not read many of its books, and in the seminary did not take a number of the standard secular courses: sociology, psychology, anthropology, perhaps not even economics or political science. His own studies were in the Latin and not in the American manner. His spirituality derives from eighteenth- and nineteenth-century spiritual and moral books, written by specifiable schools of European spiritual thought. In his parish, he does not have the dialogue Mass, nor in any noticeable way encourage the layman's use of intelligence and initiative in the Church. Furthermore, he believes it is simply wrong for a Catholic to be on a secular campus. Any Catholic there, he believes and perhaps even announces publicly, has and deserves to have problems—which he can solve on his own.

Now the students and faculty members who learn of these attitudes through his sermons can hardly help thinking of the worst accusations in their textbooks: the Church is incurably medieval, Latin, anti-intellectual, unmodern; and her priests are unread, heedless, and immovable. Compared to the understanding, generosity of mind, and creative searching which they find in their nonbelieving professors, this pastor comes off a very poor second, and not very much like Christ. The example is of course extreme, but only to make a point. The ordinary parish priest near a secular campus is undergoing a scrutiny of which he may not even be conscious, from which probably only a giant in the ways of the Lord would come off well. Still, if the younger, less stable Catholic begins to disidentify with the Church and things Catholic, and if the Catholic faculty member manifests a polite, distant frustration, the secular campus may be even less to blame than the Catholic parish.

It is true that the general picture is slowly beginning to improve. More priests seem to enter Newman work every year. One or two religious communities, like the Paulists, are entering the field more strongly. The founding of the Pittsburgh Oratory by Bishop Wright is a most hopeful event. Several former Newman chaplains are now bishops, and can no doubt be counted upon to make the needs of the campus known. But these developments are in the range of numbers still so small—three or four men here, a half-dozen there—that they are bare tokens before the magnitude of the task. And that task is becoming greater every year.

By 1970, nearly a million Catholics will be on secular campuses. Financially, private schools will be falling farther and farther behind those schools which receive tax aid. Again, Catholic schools cannot keep pace in providing personnel, even if they had the money: in the decade 1948–1958 Cornell University alone gave more doctoral degrees than all the

Catholic graduate schools put together. (Nationally, of 83,439 doctorates granted, 2,354 were granted by Catholic schools.) Still again, the United States Office of Education estimates that the cost of a college education at a private school away from home will climb from $2,500 in 1960 to $4,600 in 1970. A Catholic family with two children in college at the same time will need almost $37,000 to send both to a private school for four years. These, then, are the practical pressures influencing Catholics toward the secular campuses. Yet there is reason to believe that these pressures can have a good effect, both upon Catholicism and upon America. For, as Cardinal Gibbons and Archbishop Ireland saw even in the last century, it is well for Catholics to assimilate thoroughly the culture in which they live, and for the secular environment to feel the yeast of the Gospels. It is thus that the Church was changed by, and changed, other cultures in her history.

The present inadequate care for the half-million Catholics on secular campuses is dangerous, then, not because these Catholics might lose their faith, but because they might have no light from the Gospels to bring to the secular environment. As *America* made clear in a report in 1961, and as those with experience testify, Catholics are in no greater danger of losing their faith on a secular campus than downtown in an office or elsewhere in our secular world. The Achilles heel of American Catholicism is its fear and defensiveness; in its fear it has often not even taught the full, expansive tradition of Catholicism. Many graduates of twelve years of Catholic schooling have not ever read the Gospels through. It appears that most Catholics graduating from high school, Catholic or public, have very little insight into their faith, and have read very few creative, critical, challenging books concerning their faith. The danger is that they are not hiding very much light under their bushel, even should they lift it a little.

Yet it is the Catholic tradition, not the secularist tradition, which best explains man's moral dilemmas, and the presence of evil in the world, and the dignity of man. The movement of the nineteenth century seemed to support the secularist dream; time is not so gentle with it in our century. Indeed, the secular thinker often warns himself against a "failure of nerve," as if he and not the religious man were in danger of losing his faith. "Writers who were skeptical and uncompromising intellectuals only twenty years ago," writes Ben Ray Redman in his introduction to the Viking *Voltaire*, "are now taking refuge in old religions of the West and even older Eastern mysteries." It is true that Mr. Redman construes reason so narrowly that for him religion is a flight from reason. But the point is that it is not the believer but the unbeliever who is in danger if a living, intellectual faith comes to the campus.

As Christopher Dawson has pointed out, for the secularist who has been taught to believe that Catholicism and intellectual honesty are contradictory, encounter with a Catholic devoted to the life of intelligence requires an important and eventually far-reaching revision. The tragedy of the moment, however, is that the tradition of American Catholicism is largely anti-intellectual; beyond that, it is that few of the Catholic intellectuals already on the campuses are able to achieve much effectual "mediation."

Thus if we turn from what the American Church is doing for Catholics on secular campuses, to what Catholics there are doing for her, we face another disappointment. There are a number of outstanding Catholics on faculties all around the country. There is sometimes evidence of a new spirit in the air: as among those Catholic graduate students who by design seek employment on some campus where the percentage of Catholic instructors is particularly low, or nil. But for the most part the real dimensions of Catholic witness on a secular campus have not been appreciated. No doubt the first task is simply to get Catholics on the campuses and among the faculty. No doubt the personal presence of a Catholic in the department or on the staff is an aid to understanding, and sometimes a stimulation to curiosity. (Wonderfully humorous questions are sometimes asked; the whole jumble of Inquisition, Franco, fish on Fridays, grace, and the Irish couldn't help being incongruous.) No doubt, too, the first task of the Catholic student is to attain excellence in his field. But all of this is only the shell, perhaps only a soft sell of the image of the Church. The deeper task is intellectually to reunite the divergent cultures—the Catholic and the secular—and this task requires some effort even to define.

The ideals of the secular intellectual community are not

as Catholics sometimes stereotype them. Nearly everybody is by now clear that the secular thinker is not militantly atheistic; neither is he positively antisupernatural. He is not even cold or indifferent to religion, let alone to morality. Rather, he is caught up in his own moral enthusiasm. He is very interested in the present world, in making it a better place in which to live, in finding out what works best in it, in trying to make as many people as possible happy within it. Compared to the repressive, self-righteous ideals of some believers, the ideals of the secular thinker are often enlarging and inspiring. The uncritical Christian may, in fact, confound this admirable spirit with a kind of charity, this dedication to truth as a kind of natural faith. One cannot help being attracted by it, and sincerely emulating it.

Yet one type of secular idealism misses some of the reality of human existence: it misses sin and human moral frailty; it misses man's ontological loneliness, and dependence; it does not include in its view the vast darkness all around man. Rather, it works busily and steadily in a tiny circle of clear scientific light, or in a vaguer circle of the insights of art. The darkness closes in and snuffs one member after another from the circle of the living; one age's scientific truth is another's naiveté. A naturalist may think we can know nothing about the dark, and that faith is unreasonable, and that the historic faiths are irrevocably discredited. He does not really live in the dark. He may resolve not to let it preoccupy him, or, if he is Promethean, may shake his fist at it occasionally; but for the most part he keeps busy at his work, and his human loves, and his patronage of art and culture. His may be the contemporary form of what Pascal called man's everlasting *divertissement*: man averts his eyes from too much reality.

On the other hand, there is another type of secular thinker, much influenced by the irrationality so manifest in the events of our century, who is quite aware of evil. Like Camus, he cherishes honesty and tries to live in the "cold desert," under the "polar light" of the absurd. Such a thinker is closer in spirit to St. John of the Cross than, say, to Bishop Sheen or Norman Vincent Peale; but however close to the empty, nihilistic strain of the Catholic tradition, he does not believe. He does not trust a God in that darkness. He does not take heart from the fact of his own consciousness, the fact of communication between men and the fact of love, to extrapolate to a universal order of love, and person-to-Person communication. His universe is barren. He believes himself more honest, more courageous, more humble than the believer; though if, perhaps, he could find an honest way he, too, might believe.

The honesty of this nonbeliever is compelling. The Catholic, listening to his own silence, deprived of any of the created tokens of faith and living in inner emptiness and loneliness, is very much attracted. His heart cries out: "I too!" And yet he believes. What? Why? Who has seen God? And yet the Catholic must not fall into the trap of believing that there are two worlds, one "natural" and one "supernatural." If the confidence of busy men like John

Dewey and other *ex professo* naturalists does not tempt him, or does not seem adequate to the realities of the twentieth century, the call of the irrational in his heart is more difficult to still. Even here, however, he must return to the mystery of the cross, great act of irrationality at the heart of Christian belief, and to those data of hope experienced in human life and action which give credibility to resurrection. He dare not reify the distinction between "natural" and "supernatural," which are but abstractions. There is only this one present, concrete world in which we live. Depths of evil, irrationality, and suffering are at the heart of it, and into those depths every man must descend, so measuring his stature. Only from those depths, only after loss, can resurrection be hoped. Those who preach an easy way preach illusion.

The world in which we live is a fallen world, and a redeemed world; it was not ever a merely natural world. Facts in it keep breaking through any naturalistic interpretation; that is what makes the Christian view reasonable. The implication of the Christian view is that the secular view is an abstraction, which overlooks salient facts about man, particularly about man's inner life. The Catholic's objection to the secular thinker is not that he is too natural; it is that he has looked for, and served, an abstraction which does not exist.

The difficulty is that in his haste to acquire excellence in his field, the Catholic will accept without detecting it a discipline established around the abstraction of the purely natural man. He will keep up the practice of his faith, his moral observance, even, perhaps, his theological reading. Even to the acute observer, it will not seem that he is "secularized"; indeed, in his personal inner life he may have attained an enviable quiet and union with God. But there will still be a radical disunity in his intellectual view, unless he has adverted to, and resolved, the difference between the naturalist's image of man and his own. The resolution of this difference will make him a different kind of scholar than the secular thinker, and will mark his distinct and revolutionary contribution to his discipline. It will lead his attention to different problems, marshal to his support different insights, set him to working out new techniques. He has more to say about man than the secular thinker, and if he is faithful to his own intellectual vision, he will work out the intellectual ways of expressing it.

Another way of making this point, more concretely, is to attend to the difference between the Catholic and the secular culture which Christopher Dawson, T. S. Eliot, and Jacques Maritain have pointed out for our generation. There is a larger gap between these two cultures, and a more significant one, than between the two poles of the secular culture which C. P. Snow has pointed out. The narrow construction put on *raison*—which Blaise Pascal was to wrestle with, as must all of us since Descartes—leads inevitably to the split Sir Charles remarks. But that same narrow construction, fixed at the Renaissance, took its antireligious turn in the Enlightenment, as it takes its antihumanist

turn today. It began by favoring Galileo's "primary qualities," the "objective," the countable, the precise. It has
left out the person. Even the great secular political achievements which have favored the human person have been
subverted both by a utilitarian ethic and by a utilitarian,
technical social order. The secular ideal, perhaps in spite of
itself, makes man a technician, busy upon the walls of the
City of Man.

The profound conflict between a Catholic culture and
a secular culture is that between the man who wishes to
be a citizen both of the City of God and the City of
Man, and the man whose horizon is cut off by the walls
of the City of Man. There is reason to believe that the
cutting off of those horizons does violence to what man is.
But there is also reason to believe that the medieval and
other attempts to work out the relationships between
the two Cities were not so favored as our own, neither in
experience with several new forms of intellectual inquiry,
nor in the working out of political and social techniques
like compulsory education and democracy. If a Catholic
culture is to grow in America, it will be different from
any past Catholic culture.

The more sophisticated Catholic student on the secular campus has gotten past the stage of thinking that
the difference between the Catholic and secular culture
is a matter of apologetics; the old conflicts between religion and science, except perhaps in psychology and anthropology, are pretty well past. But if some of his defensiveness
is gone, he has not yet got to the point—in large enough

numbers at least—from which he can see the positive, creative work that lies before him. He has not yet taken matters into his own hands, and begun to create a new form of the Catholic tradition, a further growth in "the stature of Christ." His experience has shown him Catholicism in one of its particularly narrow and sectarian moments: American Catholicism to the present. Thus he may tend to have no more to do intellectually with the Church than necessary, notwithstanding his faithfulness to her discipline.

A brief glance every once in a while, over his shoulder, tells him the Church is becoming "more liberal all the time"; but he seems to leave those hard-won advances to the efforts to his French and German confrères. He seems to feel no obligation to do such creative work on his own. But perhaps it is rather that his secular discipline keeps him busy, and keeps him far away from those concerns that have to do with the personal lives of men, and hence with the life of faith. Whatever the reason, even the best of those Catholics on the secular campus are doing little as yet to create a new form of Catholic life, in the assimilation of American secular culture. That is the large task that lies ahead.

Thus the failures of the American Church in taking care of its many sons and daughters on the secular campus, its anti-intellectualism, its lack of critical, creative drive, must be paid for for some time to come. We are even hindered by a lack of clear sociological knowledge of what types of Catholic students are on secular campuses, and what the problems peculiar to each type are; at present, we must fall back on rough intuitions, even in trying to help. Again, it seems quite clear that the solution to this complex of problems cannot await the action of the clergy, for not only are there too few priests whom the bishops will free for college work, but also there are too few priests ready for such work. Seminary education is itself a chief victim of the split between the two cultures, and moreover does not always have deep roots in historic Catholic culture so much as in recent, post-Tridentine culture.

There seems no immediate remedy for the problems of the Catholic student on the secular campus except his own creative action. And in fact one hears occasionally of the spontaneous formation of small groups of Catholic graduate students and students, and even of the appearance of lively magazines or papers, like the University of Pennsylvania's *Assent*. These students can stimulate one another in the creative rediscovery of the Catholic intellectual vision. They can suggest books and articles to one another, and counteract each other's blind spots.

Meanwhile, the Newman chaplains are hopelessly overworked. It seems without a doubt that on the secular campus the layman must take care of himself. It is here, it seems, that he will come into his own. On the other hand, one great Catholic resource might be tapped to aid him: the nuns. Moreover, there seem to be ways of combining the advantages of the Catholic and the secular college, so as to bridge the present gap between them.

13 THE NUN IN THE WORLD

"Much has been written about priest-laity relationships," Cardinal Suenens has written, "but not enough has been done to integrate into this discussion the proper place of the nun." The Catholic directory for 1963 shows that there are over 175,000 nuns in the United States; that is, more than three times the number of priests, surely the greatest spiritual force in our nation. 102,000 of these sisters teach, affecting directly most of the six million students in American Catholic schools. Yet amid all the healthy self-examination among American Catholics these last ten years, very seldom have laymen had a chance to reflect on their relationship to the sisters, and the sisters' to them.

Ignazio Silone once wrote that with one hundred young men who would live chastely and poorly and dedicate themselves to the poor, he could remake Italy. American Catholic culture, however, remains quite timid, uncreative, legalistic, even though not one hundred but scores of thousands of young men and young women give their substance, their youth, their lives to evangelical vows. Why is there such a gap between the good will of novices and the general effect of their later lives? It is possible to read the Gospels and the Acts of the Apostles, close one's eyes, and find it difficult to apply the descriptions of the primitive Christians to American religious, even though these religious show great good will. The observer does not often get a sense of freedom, creativity, social consciousness, joy, from the religious he meets. He gets rather (it must be confessed) the sense of organization, tiredness, professionalism, the piety of brochures and building-fund campaigns.

Undoubtedly, the nuns do work for which American Catholics cannot be grateful enough. Yet it is difficult for a layman to feel joy on seeing a young woman enter the convent, even when he is in favor of her decision. He is more apt to feel admiration, anxiety, hope. He cannot be sure that she is entering a life of new spiritual freedom, where she will find help and encouragement in discovering the depths of the human spirit. He hopes she will find courage to be faithful under the great strains of convent life in our generation. the heavy schedules, the technical preoccupations, the conflicts between older and newer ideals, the pouring of twentieth-century tasks and pace into the institutional forms of a more leisurely day. The layman cannot help feeling that the sisterhoods add unnecessary strain to the contemporary living of the Gospels. When many of the present sisterhoods were founded, the day's work ended with sundown, the electric light was not in use, and it was no doubt relaxing to sit in a circle at evening recreation, quietly stitching, and attempting "edifying discourse." It must be difficult for the sister of today to find peace in a convent caught between two conflicting social orders.

Thus the fear voiced by the layman is very different from the opposition encountered by Teresa of Avila when she wished to enter the convent. It is not that the young girls entering the sisterhoods are "leaving the world" and entering on a life too evangelical, too ideal. It is rather that they may be kept from the Gospels by institutional forms and attitudes that are in the throes and confusion of change. The girl who enters the convent in our generation is in for an adventurous, trying life, whose future she may help shape, but whose conflicts will certainly render her own peace uneven.

On such matters, it is difficult for the layman to make clear his relationship with the sisters. For too many years there has been a breakdown in candor in American Catholic life. The clergy fear to say things that might scandalize the laity; the religious who administer colleges are often very secretive vis-à-vis their lay faculty; laymen scarcely ever say to religious what they most deeply think and feel. There is a conspiracy of gentility, politeness, and adulation, which inhibits honest sentiment and direct speech; and these conventions carry over from the speakers' platform and the Catholic press to private conversations. A layman finds only a few priests or religious to whom he would confide the same convictions, doubts, criticisms he confides quite readily to many laymen. This conspiracy against candor is apparent to the impulsive and the naturally frank within the Catholic environment; and those who live outside that environment sense again the air of quaintness, constraint, and less-than-truth when, on occasion, they are called back into it.

But with American sisters it is, in general, particularly hard to be honest. The layman cannot help admiring the heroism of their lives; moreover, the better he knows them, the more he recognizes how desperately they try to be worthy brides of Christ. But the sisters seem so sheltered from secular life as it is now lived, that one does not know by which standard to judge them, theirs or one's own. Still again, they spend so much of their lives in the company of children, or at most among girls of college age, that the layman soon finds himself speaking gently and in circumlocutions. Perhaps in spite of himself, the layman cannot help wanting to shelter nuns from the full facts, or from the full force of his own convictions, objections, or feelings. Isn't it always unfair, by the nineteenth-century code, to argue with a lady? And surely, to enter conversation with most nuns is to accept the conventions of that code, however unusual among other women of our century.

The layman can't help feeling that the sister, once formed by novitiate and juniorate into the convent code, and then kept isolated by her rule from free mingling with the men and women of our society, slowly adopts as the normal way of viewing the world the imperatives and the delicatenesses she has been taught to observe. Her mentors may think of these as particularly civilizing, as leaven in a harsher and more vulgar world, as a genteel tradition worth preserving. But if this is the choice that nuns in America make, they should realize that it deprives them of the chance for leadership; it robs them of positive spiritual force, with its multiplier-effect among their students; it makes them, not apostles, but guardians; it takes them out of the mainstream and the center of the fray and—to use the harsh, honest word—it makes their work defensive and ephemeral. Men and women in the secular world cannot live by the conventions of a bygone day; many leave much of their Catholic training at the school door.

The layman, of course, realizes that a great number of American sisters have already seen the dilemmas of the modern nun. Some sisters in every community, and certain sisterhoods from among others, are far advanced in creating a new style of sanctity, work, and life for nuns—a style peculiarly American and peculiarly of our century. Moreover, the Sister Formation Movement has given such sisters a national focus of stimulation and energy. With a national office in Washington, an ambitious program of publications, conferences, and lectures, the SFM also publishes a *Bulletin* which for several years was a pacesetter in translating into English the creative new theology of the religious life which has been stirring in Europe. Thus in several respects, the movement toward *aggiornamento* was already farther along among American nuns than among American brothers or priests even before the Vatican Council.

In an invaluable book, however, of which nuns in this country are already making wide use, Cardinal Suenens (*The Nun in the World*, Newman paperback), notes that sisters are still treated by canon law and ecclesiastical traditions as minors, looked on as in need of protection, not as mature persons of equal stature with men. Many individual nuns, of course, have earned respect from clergy and laity as mature, competent equals; but nuns in general have not yet won equality. The great contribution made by Cardinal Suenens is to have put the present situation of the nuns in historical, spiritual, and sociological context; he has been frank and has at last given public voice to the conflicts and difficulties many sisters have suffered. He has emphasized that sisters need not conceive of themselves as defenders of the faith or preservers of a more gentle tradition, but as apostles who can belong to and help shape the secular world. He has emphasized that the natural role for sisters is among the women of the twentieth century, and has urged the sisters to enter the adult, secular world.

Such encouragement is sorely needed. The ordinary layman in America, educated or uneducated, does not look on the sisters as leaders of great relevance to our secular life. He entrusts his children to the sisters with affection and gratitude, and knows that the work the sisters do in the schools (not to mention in the hospitals and homes) is without price. At the same time, he is not likely to take the sisters critically or seriously. Adult laymen rarely converse with sisters, question them, challenge them, argue with them. Even the poorly educated layman takes it as his prerogative to smile on some of the sisters' regulations, their attitudes, some of the things they say. No doubt the children in school occasionally give evidence of these attitudes from the home.

There are two important respects in which the layman tends to think the life of the sister is remote from his. I have already stressed the first one, the all-embracing attitude of obedience and gentility shaped by a life entirely under the authority of superiors, regulations, and the convent code. This attitude is not inspiring to the layman. Nor does it seem like the attitude of the primitive Christians; it seems, rather, the result of several post-Tridentine cultural forces, which have given the Gospels an unnecessary twist.

The second question is that of womanhood and sex. American sisters sometimes convey an ethereal impression: of women trying hard to live as though they were "spiritual creatures," as though they didn't need affection and were "above" sex. One might think of American nuns as ladies, hardly as women. They do not seem to be of earth, and the general impression they give is perhaps rather Jansenist than Christian; their chastity seems negative and unreal, rather than passionate and alive. The strictures that nuns sometimes impose on girls who wear the normal touch of lipstick becoming to their age, or the conventional shorts and necklines of our country and time, do not seem Christian or wise. Correspondingly, the fears and uncertainties concerning sex felt by many of the girls who graduate from Catholic schools are scarcely due to Christian modesty alone, which need have no fear; they seem due to the sexual uncertainties of their teachers (and parents).

On these two matters, as well as on many others, two trained Jesuit psychologists, John J. Evoy and Van F. Christoph, *Personality Development in the Religious Life* (Sheed & Ward), join Cardinal Suenens in making the year of the Vatican Council a turning point in publications for American nuns. On the matter of obedience, surely the area of greatest abuse among American sisters, this book makes an invaluable contribution. It details the psychological risks inherent in the superior-subject relationship; it discusses the aberrations that can lurk in rigidity, docility, self-sacrifice—wherever self-knowledge and intelligence are excluded. It speaks a great deal of affection and appreciation.

Cardinal Léger of Montreal has also added a long, pointed pastoral: *La Religieuse Enseignante Aujourd'hui.* The emphasis here, as in the other books, is on secularization, in the positive sense of that word: becoming more apostolic, becoming more human. Historically, this shift in emphasis marks a return to the biblical, liturgical, apostolic spirituality of the early ages of the Church, as distinct from the self-centered and defensive spirituality of a later tradition.

This shift is crucial, because under that later tradition it was very difficult for the sensitive and inquiring nun to understand herself as a human being, or to share the nat-

uralness of the Gospels and of the great religious humanists
like Teresa of Avila and John of the Cross. The spiritual
reading conventional in American convents and seminaries
since their post-Tridentine origins—reading which gave
Thérèse of Lisieux headaches—has been much affected
by the individualism and militarism of the Counter Reformation. It often stresses the pharisaic virtues of observance, self-perfection, unquestioning obedience, even as it
warns against their dangers; and this stress coupled with
the counterwarnings against it often produces disquiet and
anxiety. The more devoted a "soul" is (rather than a
"person"), the more impossible perfection seems and the
more imperative it seems never to relax, not even for a
moment—for it is just then that corruption strikes. Nuns
of today carry staggering work loads; many sisters face
thirty-five hours of teaching a week, plus a turn at cooking
supper at home, plus prayers and housecleaning, and after-
school and weekend catechetical assignments. Sister is not
allowed to stop for a nap, or to take recreation except at
specified times, in specified ways. She rarely has a chance
to be alone. To further harry her inner life with the metic-
ulous concepts of Counter-Reformation spirituality is to
add a cruel torture, and take her peace.

Cardinal Suenens has underlined the concept of enclosure as the key point in rethinking the role of the sisters
in the future. It is a mistake, he thinks, to model the sisterhoods on monastic forms. Sisters belong to the secular
world, and the secular world to them; it is among men that

they will find their Love. The real thrust in the work of the great founders of religious communities in the seventeenth to nineteenth centuries was that of beginning the long path back to the authentic tradition of the early Church, the path that leads from Trent to the Second Vatican Council and beyond. They were the ones who achieved the first partial insights into the needs of the new Church of the industrial, democratic, pluralistic state. It would be a mistake to be faithful to the moment of history in which they reached their insight, instead of to the further development of that insight in history.

Thus, Cardinal Suenens argues, the greatest need of the present is to humanize Christianity, a need more urgent than that of Christianizing secular humanism. The Church is in the world, redemption is for men; there is no natural world, no "corrupt" world; the world is already redeemed. Catholicism must begin to live these humanizing (or divinizing) truths again; it is especially important that this life be begun in America. In many respects, American Catholicism is becoming the center of the Church universal, and what happens here is of the utmost importance for the shape of the future world culture.

If the sisters of America, therefore, were to opt for Cardinal Suenen's conception of their vocation, the impetus they would give to the humanization of Catholicism in the world would be immeasurable. No one in America is in the position to give the symbolic, sweeping impetus which the 175,000 sisters could give. Every step the nuns take in the present *aggiornamento* has a dramatic effect on the ordinary layman; the nuns are a very visible part of the Church. Changes in their regulations, habits, attitudes, methods, affect many millions. But the truly fundamental question is: How much effect do nuns wish to have on the secular world?

The sisters could multiply their effectiveness, for example, by rethinking their commitment to the parochial schools. About half our Catholic children are in public schools; do they need the sisters less than others? Cadres of sisters could be trained in contemporary liturgical and social catechetics to teach all Catholic children, in public as in parochial schools. The sisters in the parochial schools could concentrate on theology and social action, leaving algebra and geography and history to the laymen. Above all, the sisters should stress social action; this is the unsurpassed way to teach the Gospels. Weren't most of our sisters' communities founded among the poor, for the oppressed? In America these same communities have often become institutionalized, proper, and safe. The nuns are not thought of as poor, but middle class.

Without question, racial violence is rising toward the eruption point in our northern cities, precisely in the very population centers where convents are most concentrated: Boston, New York, Chicago, Philadelphia, Detroit. There is no group in America better fitted to play the part of intercession, justice, peace, and love, in the Negro neighborhoods than the sisters from these convents. The effect on the large Catholic populations in these cities of sisters who take the part of the Negro, who protest with him, who march with him, who help his wife and children in their many emotional and economic needs, is overpowering. But often the nuns seem politely remote from the cries for justice; there is a discrepancy between their grasp of reality and that of many of their foundresses.

The entrance of the sisters in the world, which Cardinal Suenens urges, will not take place until the sisters cease to be afraid: evidencing their fear in going out two by two, locking doors, treating the convent as an enclosure out of the storms. The noise and anguish of city streets has got to enter convent windows, if the sisters are to help the sons of men. But even within the existing institutions, the local parish and parochial school, the nuns could do much more mingling with the adult world. The Parent's Days at school are at present innocuous, dishonest affairs, at which neither sisters, pastor, nor parents truly speak their minds to one another. Laymen should be allowed to speak frankly about the policies and goals of the school, and sisters should be able to challenge in return.

Moreover, it is surely a mistake for sisters to limit their labors in the parish only to the children. Why are not some sisters, at least, prepared to lead discussion groups on Scripture, liturgy, social action among adults? Such sisters would need to be prepared to argue and discuss, in the manner of the secular world. More effectively than any one else, they could bring the encyclicals of the recent popes into ordinary parish life where they are not now attended to. Such a program might mean that the sisters would have to leave the convent in the evenings, and take part in meetings in the homes of parishioners. If the young girls of the Confraternity of Christian Doctrine can do such work, why can't sisters? Only changeable traditions stand in the way.

Finally, groups of the most intelligent and sensitive nuns, who are already intolerably restless in grammar and high schools, could be trained for a new kind of work on secular campuses, where five-eighths of Catholic undergraduates are in attendance. Even a half-dozen sisters—theologians, poets, historians, painters—would give a great cultural lift to Catholic women on campus. The sisters could lecture, counsel, guide reading programs, help with research papers, direct social action, encourage ecumenical encounters, provide a haven for retreat and recollection. Groups of students from Harvard and Radcliffe, for example, drive over a hundred miles regularly, to come under the marvelous influence of the nuns of Regina Laudis convent in Connecticut.

Each of these suggestions, of course, can be weighed only by the sisters themselves, according to what they wish to do with their lives. But there is no questioning how profound a reconsideration is called for; it is not this or that detail, it is the very self-conception of the sisters which is at stake. No doubt those nuns who already have contact with secular education have a new perspective on their lives. It is apparently a salutary shock to move from a climate where sisters are unquestioned queens to one in which the Catholic ghetto is only a small part of the world. The important point is for increasingly more nuns to see themselves as they are seen.

The impact of argument, advice, criticism, discussion, from contact with lay adults, and also with non-Catholics and nonbelievers, will have deep repercussions on the sister's understanding of her own vocation, and on her sense of belonging to all men. The vocation problem will be relieved; girls will at least no longer feel they are leaving for a strange world, but for adult tasks that will extend and enrich their willing spirits. Moreover, the benefits that would redound on laymen, and ultimately on American culture as a whole, would be surpassingly great. Every nun who enters the stream of American life, who enters on the side of justice and liberty, will draw in her wake the dozens of laymen she teaches or influences and the hundreds who see her. The Gospels will then, at last, begin to permeate, with their sense of purpose and poverty and joy, the apathy of so much of American middle-class life.

14 CATHOLIC and SECULAR

Nuns are not the only ones who will benefit by secularization, in the positive sense of that word. Perplexed parents looking ahead to the choice of a college for their sons or daughters often ask: "How does Catholic education compare to education in a secular college?" Students on a Catholic campus sometimes ask: "Are we missing anything by not being on a secular campus?" Students on a secular campus, less often, ask the reverse. The questions reveal that there are, at present, two different "worlds" for the Catholic in America, the Catholic world and the secular world. The interpenetration of these worlds is, surely, both the healthy and the inevitable course of the future. In many areas of the country, even now, there is no conclusive reason why a student should not have the best of both worlds, if educators cared enough to make it possible.

Before reflecting on the possibilities before us, however, it might be well to characterize the present gap between the two worlds. Simple contrasts like "godless" against "God-fearing," or "secularistic" against "divinely given," or "materialistic" against "spiritual," do not do justice to the actual differences. Not all in Catholic schools fear God, live by the spirit, understand the Gospels; many in non-Catholic schools do. Many men on a secular campus may not believe in God; but it is difficult for those of lesser moral stature to find fault with their nobility of character or fidelity to conscience. Nor is it so clear, as commencement oratory in Catholic colleges would have us believe, that Catholic colleges are the repositories of the Western tradition, while the secular colleges are slowly emptying it out upon the ground.

It is a striking testament to the present division into two worlds that the American clergy regularly denounce the waves of "secularism" rising ever higher in our land, while publicly professed nonbelievers bewail, instead, the rising tide of belief. Thus Paul Edwards explicitly edited Bertrand Russell's *Why I Am Not a Christian* as an attempt to stem the flood of the religious revival; Walter Kaufmann, similarly hurried out his *Critique of Religion and Philosophy*; Sidney Hook wrote in his essay, "The New Failure of Nerve," that "large sections of the intellectuals and clerks of the Western world are abandoning the hard-won critical positions of the last few centuries." Who ought to feel discouraged? Is the crisis in which we live one of belief or of nonbelief?

On the philosophical plane, the age in which we live seems characterized by a greater openness and honesty than has been felt for many generations. It is abundantly clear that medieval philosophy cannot be lifted up in a bundle, wholesale, and carried into the twentieth century. At the same time, a certain humility is coming over rival philosophies. Positivism has floundered over difficulties with its own basic principle; naturalists are chided by their confrères for an optimism, neither proper to our generation nor critically founded; existentialists have difficulty communicating to those who do not share their mood; linguistic analysts are sensitive to the criticism that they deal in no more than trivialities. Thus in a hiatus during which each school is seeing to its own difficulties, a ripe pluralism is in effect. Ours is a good time for mutual stimulation and creativity.

Moreover, on the institutional plane, the gap between the two worlds is not so great as it once was. The lay faculties at Catholic colleges have come to outnumber the clerics on the faculty by three or even five to one. A large number of these laymen received their degrees from secular colleges, as have increasing numbers of the priests and nuns. In many Catholic colleges, an increasing number of non-Catholic professors are being hired. There is no reason why an increasing number of non-Catholic students are not encouraged to attend them too.

All these influences are fruitful. On the college level a good education is a pluralistic education; in a university a student should encounter a universal range of views.

Thus many of the classes on a Catholic campus are very like their counterparts on a secular campus. The same basic sources are read; the same methods are used; the same standards are maintained. Catholics do not yet appear to have schools to rank with the dozen or so best secular schools, though the best students in several Catholic colleges might well gain a competence comparable to what is available in the best secular schools. Generally, the best Catholic colleges appear to rank with the better of the second-ranked secular schools, a cut above the average state college campus.

The advantage of the Catholic campus is its comparative religious sophistication. Both from his campus environment and from professional classroom work, the student on a Catholic campus is likely to have a more highly developed religious sense than the student on a secular campus. He will have read more about religion, learned more methods proper to religious inquiry, and practiced more. On the other hand, he is likely to have a less highly developed respect for other religious or even antireligious points of view. And he will not have had the experience of criticizing his own religious points of view from within a different intellectual horizon.

The concept of horizon is an important one in education. Literally, a horizon is a maximum field of vision from a determinate standpoint; Lonergan first applied the concept to philosophy. In education, horizon is a metaphor for the personal, subjective pole of human judgment and its relation to information and facts. The chief drawback of a Catholic education is that the frame of judgment appears to be all-too-determinate. The student gets too used to looking at matters from one point of view. He may thereby miss much of their variety and range, and many of their alternative explanations. The horizon on a secular campus, on the other hand, may at first glance appear to lack structure at all. Then, on second glance, it may appear to offer a distinctive structure, the "secularist" point of view. But neither of these glances is accurate. The secular campus provides an arena for free, unstructured discussion; within that arena, one party may gain ascendancy for a time, as naturalists and pragmatists appear to have done at present. But whatever the ascendant power, its program does not achieve the status of official dogma; its reign invites reversal; its very becoming established renders it suspect to the quick and the discerning. Without attempting in any institutional way to achieve the "synthesis" of which Catholic colleges boast so much, the secular university seems in fact to promote, through the method of liberty, the achievement of a profound personal synthesis in a remarkable number of its graduates.

This difference in method seems to have profound psychic roots. Catholic pastoral theory seems clearly to favor the weak, the slow, the undiscerning; the criterion for every move seems to be whether it protects the majority. On the contrary, the secular theorist favors the strong, the bright, the critical. Oliver Wendell Holmes, much closer to Darwin than our generation is, put the issue bluntly in terms of the survival of the fittest; his motivation in his scholarly work was to be the best. Correspondingly, academic competition on a secular campus is much more fierce than on a Catholic campus. In the latter, everything favors the average guy who does what he's told; in the former, the rewards go to those who achieve.

There are two other main differences between the secular and the Catholic horizon. The first has to do with access to information, the other to criteria of relevance and evidence. The student on the secular campus will scarcely get to read Newman, Maritain, Claudel, Undset, Greene. When he does sample them, they will be in the company of John Stuart Mill, Sartre, Gide, Joyce, Ayer, Camus; and in this company they may well seem peripheral. On the Catholic campus, on the other hand, "the great tradition" will preoccupy the student's time. No matter how important an author appears on the contemporary scene, if he stands outside that tradition he is viewed as aberrant. "Catholic" figures, together with sympathizers like Dostoevsky, Berdyaev, Eliot, Toynbee, and even Baudelaire, are likely to dominate the horizon. Catholic figures will be read to be admired; non-Catholics to be baptized or refuted. When a Catholic graduate goes to a secular graduate school, he will therefore have a fund of information not shared by his non-Catholic fellows; but he will also have difficulty in catching up on their world of references. Even the information he already has, he will have to reassimilate from another point of view before he will be able to communicate it.

Where prior standards of relevance and evidence are different, subsequent evaluation of data is bound to be. St. Thomas may weigh heavily on a Catholic campus, but on a secular campus he is one among very many other philosophers, one who, moreover, was sufficiently a creature of his times to allow heretics to be burned at the stake. Again, different matters are laughing matters on one campus than another; to non-Christians, some Christian beliefs seem amusing, just as to believers some hopes of secular thinkers seem naive. Different topics may be emphasized, different principles prized, different methods of argument favored, different evidence accepted. The student may well acquire different mental and emotional habits on the one campus than on the other.

On this point, it might be comforting to believe that "the Catholic mind" is the more accurate one, and that "the others" fall short of certain standards. But what is "the Catholic mind"? If a Council is needed to "bring the Church up to date," how long has the Church needed reforming? In that period of the Church, who best spoke for the "real" spirit of the Church, Bishop X, Father Y, philosopher Z, lay journalist Q? True enough, the ordinary teaching of the Church is the office of bishops and pastors. But what if these men fall behind the leadership of Rome, or Rome behind theirs? What if there are various schools of thought among bishops and pastors, not on the propositions of the creed but on the horizon within which these are to be viewed? The glory of Pope John's session of the Vatican Council was its freedom of discussion. It seemed in that session that the Catholic mind is not something clear and already achieved, but something to be worked out through the rigors of open argument, even on fundamental questions of horizon.

Moreover, since it appears that the intellectual horizon of American Catholics has been excessively limited and unluminous in the past, that even in theology Americans have produced next to nothing, it seems clear that the "American Catholic mind," at any rate, cannot claim unmodified respect. Given the traditional defensiveness and apologetic attitude of American Catholicism, a neutral observer might expect that the "American Catholic mind" would not in all respects be perfectly adjusted to the facts. Occasionally, at any rate, it might try to "put the facts in a Catholic perspective," or "give the Catholic slant" on a given matter. This "mind" might offer footnotes gleaned from tradition or some authority to support its views. But among those outside the tradition, these footnotes might carry very little weight. They would find the Catholic position "interesting," perhaps, as an example of how disparate man's values are. The "Catholic mind" even if its possessors could be clearly named, does not seem universally convincing.

Moreover, great as the man is, Catholic colleges seem too much dominated by Aquinas. Every philosopher is at the mercy of those who expound his thought, all the more so if they claim to represent him. It is possible that more harm is done to Aquinas and less justice done his insights in some Catholic schools than in some secular schools. One hears too often of uncritical, imperceptive presentations of Aquinas, which leave with students the memory of arid logic and credulous dogmatism. Nothing could be farther from the achievement of that great, free, original mind. Nowadays, of course, it is in the air for everyone to be "broadminded:" it would be rare to find a Catholic professor of philosophy or theology who wasn't trying to be fair. But openness is relative, and the limits set on the inquiring mind by the faithful use of Scholastic terminology, viewpoints, and arguments can systematically block contemporary insight. A much more fruitful approach to the central traditional insights might be charted through the study of the contemporary analysis of language, Dewey, and the existentialists, with only supplementary study of Aristotle and Aquinas.

The advantage of a student spending part of his life on a secular campus is that he there comes into contact with the minds, values, and ideas which most move others in his generation. More important, he there lives in an horizon different than his own, which stretches his own and compels him to deepen and broaden it. From a cultural point of view, the life of such a student is one more living thread binding the two separate worlds closer together, incarnating the Gospels in the world. The disadvantage of attendance at a secular school, of course, is that he there learns very little of the distinctive, rich Catholic tradition. To learn of Aquinas, for example, only what Walter Kaufmann presents in his books is to learn a grotesque distortion; and to have to plow through Pegis' Modern Library Selections, or through the pocket *Summa Contra Gentiles*, on one's own is to risk confusion, disappointment, and frustration in what might be the profoundest and richest of intellectual experiences.

Nevertheless, the problem of the two worlds in education is only a microcosm of the general cultural problem. American society suffers from the inadequacy of Catholic intellectual and cultural contributions; American society does not hear the faith of Catholics effectively. Prejudices die hard; defensiveness thaws slowly. On the local level, Catholics still seem to lack a sense of civic responsibility; they confine their social obligations to their parishes: putting up the parish school, attending parish meetings. On the academic level, the Catholic reflex is to read with an eye for heresy, always on guard. Moreover, the Catholic tends to see all nonbelievers as a monolithic bloc. He does not distinguish the frank, naturalistic, exploratory nihilism of Norman Mailer, James Jones, and James Baldwin from the comfortable, urbane, optimistic skepticism of Sidney Hook, Oliver Wendell Holmes, and British philosophy. From these, he does not distinguish the Stoic, pragmatic pessimism of many in public life. He lumps all of them as "secularists."

One other feature of Catholic intellectual life in America is the abundance and persistence of Catholic gossip. A cocktail party at a Catholic college, or convention, or conference, is dominated by conversations about ecclesiastical events and personages. The imaginations of even the best seem preoccupied with the institutional structure of Catholicism. The speech of almost everyone is anticlerical, playfully or bitterly; even priests and nuns are anticlerical. The "Catholic mind" appears to have degenerated into the ecclesiastical mind. By contrast, a cocktail party in a secular environment is open on the world, more pluralistic, more respectful, more favorable to the individual talent. There is, perhaps, more egoism, an equal amount of griping about the local scene, but far less confinement to a churchy perspective.

The greatest weakness of the Catholic educational system, then, is its isolation; and such a weakness among Catholics harms Americans as a whole. Moreover, there is no need for this isolation to continue indefinitely. In recent years there has been much discussion about the experiment of St. Michael's College in Toronto, a Catholic college affiliated with a state university. No American group seems to have taken the project beyond the talking stage; yet surely the conception is a promising one. Given the countless religious communities eager to enter the educational field, but short of personnel to staff an entire college, and short of funds for paying first-class salaries, what conception is more obvious?

Catholic colleges affiliated to a secular university could offer on an ecumenical basis the very courses which many of these universities now seek; viz., courses in Christian theology and in the study of Christian culture. At the same time, students enrolled in these colleges could be taking other classes in the other colleges of the university. Instead of training their personnel in every imaginable field, religious communities could, moreover, concentrate in those fields closest to their own vocation, in Christian theology, art, and philosophy. Everyone would benefit. Christian intellectual life would be present on the secular campus by a doubly professional witness: experts in the theory of Christianity who at the same time would be bound by vow to live it perfectly.

An alternative and more gradual way of solving these same problems is to encourage the cross-registration of students in already existing Catholic and secular colleges. There is no conclusive reason, for example, why students enrolled at N.Y.U. could not attend St. John's or Fordham for some classes in theology, or why students at the latter could not attend other classes at the former. Some secular colleges like Swarthmore and Haverford, and Amherst and Smith, are already using the program of cross-registration quite effectively. In metropolitan centers, cross-registration appears to be the most practical program for giving students "the best of both worlds."

A third method of Catholic and secular interpenetration is to make more extensive use of the Newman Clubs. At present these clubs are already offering classes, or at least lectures, for Catholic students. They are handicapped by lack of man power, by lack of funds, and sometimes by lack of understanding. They are treated as a stopgap measure, sometimes as a gesture toward helping Catholic students who "shouldn't be on a secular campus anyway." But in fact the Newman Clubs are the most fruitful institution available to the American Church. If they were staffed by even some of the priests and nuns who are at present teaching biology, chemistry, French, or economics, or acting as prefects or counselors on Catholic campuses, they could offer a visible witness to Christianity in the place where it is needed most, in the seed-bed of the secular life of this land. Religion would not then seem so irrelevant to many of our young. Catholics would not seem so strange. The tradition of the religious vows would become familiar. Priests and nuns, moreover, who were assigned to work at secular campuses would themselves be obliged to widen the horizons of the seminary, convent, and even Catholic environment. They would have to think out their way of life in terms comprehensible to contemporary culture, just to make themselves understood.

Moreover, for professional scholars there is no substitute for actual daily contact with minds who habitually live in other horizons than one's own. It does not suffice for an understanding of a theology or a philosophy not one's own to read about it in books. A philosophy or a theology does not live in books; it cannot be totally expressed in a series of propositions. A philosophy or a theology is first of all a tradition and a horizon, a set of criteria of relevance and evidence; and these are usually inarticulate. It is only the lived horizon which gives meaning to the propositions of the articulated system. Thus, while pragmatism or existentialism are as easy to refute upon paper as Scholasticism, daily contact with minds who live these doctrines soon teaches one a subtlety and richness that escape the limited number of pages in a book. If American Catholic intellectual life is at present too bookish in its understanding of other ways of life, the vitalization of the many hundreds of Newman Clubs as active centers of scholarship would very quickly change the intellectual climate.

Such a project requires money; but not more money than the building of a new Catholic college. It also requires man power; but less man power than the staffing of a new Catholic college. Most of all, it requires understanding between educators on the secular campuses and their Catholic counterparts. It is part of the vicious circle that must be broken that the lack of contact between these two groups prevents the kind of action which would begin to heal it.

PART THREE

A CHRISTIAN EMPIRICISM

15 PATTERNS OF VISION

In Chapter Four, we reached a preliminary description of a Christian empiricism; in each other chapter we have tried to come to grips with another aspect of such an approach to human life. It is time now, in this final chapter, to become more explicit about the theory of knowing which is involved. This book is not yet a technical exposition; such a project will have to wait. (Bernard Lonergan's Insight[1] made many of the breakthroughs for such a study; but the front on which he was immediately fighting was not that of English and American philosophy; the battle there has barely been joined.) What is possible in the pages remaining to us is several direct sorties whose purpose, though each moves in a different direction, is to elucidate the nature and possibilities of their one same starting point. Attention ought to be focused on the starting place: on questions of attitude and method, rather than on the details of the actual exercise. Moreover, the reader will do even better if he reflects, while reading, more on his own attitudes and methods than on the words of the page. He should not, in

[1] Longmans, Green, 1957; 2nd edition, 1958.

short, make the mistake of the linguistic philosophers, whose primary interest lies in words. He should try to discover those methods and habits of mind of his which greatly affect his views and his abilities to understand or sympathize, but which do not go easily, if at all, into words. It is fruitful for a philosopher to reflect upon his own inarticulate habits so that in the discovery of himself he may begin to understand his relation to the world.

When a man turns toward the past facts or the present tasks of history, it matters a great deal into which focus he casts his mind. The facts and tasks remain the same, no matter who regards them. But the level of advantage from which they are regarded throws them and their implications into countless arrangements of shadow and light; the focus through which they are regarded alters their size and even their order. This much is obvious. But it is also possible to distinguish some patterns of vision into which a man's practical judgment will slide more or less consistently. Such investigation, in all areas of human knowing and chiefly in his own experience, is the primary task of the philosopher.

A non-Catholic friend of mine, at that time an officer in the Strategic Air Command, found it extremely difficult to reconcile his conscience, or even to clarify his conscience, concerning the policy of nuclear deterrence. He admired the devotion shown in the round-the-clock feints toward Moscow, the organization, the seriousness, the skill. "Politics," he wrote, "is the science of power. It is as objective and factual as the physical sciences. Introduce morality, and its utopian outlook will bring everything crashing down about us. Morality is for the individual. What is life without morality? And yet, there is no place for it in politics. This must sound horribly Machiavellian. But didn't even Christ leave to Caesar . . . ?"

This man rejects the simplistic moral solution of the preachers—that the answer lies in the hearts of men. One of the givens of the political situation is that the hearts of men are not reliable. Given modern power, one man's weakness may be every man's grave. Yet for him the moral solution is folly, not because it is founded on a simplistic slogan, but because it is utopian. The preacher recognizes sin and preaches penance and amendment. But what he confounds is term and potency. He is ever sliding unconsciously into eschatology while the world is still in the throes of uncompleted history. He is forever telling the individual he should act perfectly in such or such respect, whereas the whole point to moral life is that it can only gradually be achieved. Preachers and moralists soon become tired and misanthropic if they overlook the time required for moral growth; they preach as if men are, or should be, rational animals from the instant they come of age. Aristotle knew we must be satisfied with a "tincture of virtue." And Romano Guardini has written that we ought not to call ourselves Christians, but those who are striving to become so.

On the other hand, my friend was thrust into the position of denying the possibility of morality in politics: politics is power. He shrank from this conclusion with repugnance. It led to these reflections: "The Russians were justified in grinding into Budapest with their tanks. They had no choice. The integrity of the empire depended on stamping out every ember or rebellion, lest other satellites be tempted."

In this man's dilemma, then, we have isolated two basic patterns of vision: the idealist is tempted to succumb to the man of expedience; the "Quiet American" is tempted to ruthlessness. My friend vacillates between the two patterns of vision, and he resolves the dilemma only by dividing himself. On the one hand, he will live as exemplary a private life as he can; on the other, he will let society be the arena of power, and only pray that the Machiavellis of his time be mild. For him, as for most of us, the attraction of a private Walden Pond is nearly unbearable. But unable to be faithful to our logic, we remain in society, leading a life that is not life, guilty as free men for the abuses of power perpetrated in the name of the people or the corporations of which we are members. We are reduced to hoping that our cooperation is not grievous, that our guilt is not too heavy, that our inadequacy is not due to negligence or criminal mistake. What could we do, alone?

Will Herberg has remarked that the liberal is essentially utopian. If in politics, then, the liberal inclines toward the politics of power, we might expect his idealism to be especially acute in some other area of human life. It is, as soon as he begins to reflect about the Church. My friend, for example, argues somewhat like this: "Initially, the Church seems so promising; it stirs the heart with what it might do. It would win me instantly, if we did not have history to show us what can happen. Organization, selfishness, corruption—the Church is a creature of history, not a creator of a better world. I am probably a confirmed idealist, but . . ."

Again, between idealism and expedience, my friend has no third alternative. "I must sound dreadfully Machiavellian," he had written about his views on politics. There he worried about being too realistic; here about being too idealistic. He seems to want another alternative, but has none. He is caught in the schizophrenia of our time: to exercise the "useless passion" of idealism in private, and then to face political facts brutally. "Brutally" is a key word, for of course both these patterns of vision are inhuman. Jacques Maritain long ago named one, after Descartes, the "angelic temptation;" the other is Pascal's beast. Nietzsche and Hitler are plausible after Descartes and Hegel. The devastation of Hungary is not a surprising path for the messianic Russian bear.

The inadequacy of the first two patterns of vision leads to a search for a new starting point. Men have got to make an effort to create a way of looking at the world that rises above the other two, that regards all the individual and social facts without dividing the beholder. This new pattern cannot be found between the other two. A halfway point, the view of "moderates," is an evasion; it solves nothing;

it merely cringes in the middle of the road for safety; it makes no one more a man.

Usually we think of the "angelic temptation" as an extreme; but it is more revealing to look at it as a compromise. It does not go far enough; it takes the easy way. Its virtue is that it values intelligence; it manifests a thirst for an ordered, moral existence. But it fails to believe that intelligence is capable of piercing the imponderables of real, concrete history, or can reach the mixed intelligibility of the given social and political order. Therefore, it in effect abandons this present world for a vision of a better one. It does not see that there *is* an order in the incomplete world in which we live, but not an order already existing, laid up in heaven, "Which if once we gazed upon, my beloved, we should die of love and longing." It is, rather, an order to be created. The idealist does not recognize that history is in motion, is never at a perfectly intelligible term (a heaven, a paradise on earth), but nonetheless is evolving among possibilities that are intelligible, whose actuation requires human courage and intelligence, under the providence of God. The evolution of history is imperfect, uncertain, laden with risk, error, and failure. Some possibilities diminish with every choice made and every stride taken; new ones become more probable. Unintelligent and malicious actions throw into the process factors that are correspondingly incomprehensible, inviting equally malicious and unintelligent responses in return. Thus the pattern of actual history seems more irrational than rational. The idealist finds the labor of intelligence too arduous in such a world. Though he starts by esteeming intelligence, he will not go so far as to do its required work. He lacks intellectual courage.

The man of expedience is not more virtuous. He has a penchant for facing facts, but his kind of facts. He understands only his kind of rationality; he has cut intelligence down to his size. He cannot understand the logic of the Hungarian patriot of eleven who carries bottles of gasoline with himself into the tracks of a Stalin tank. Images for the Hitlers or Mussolinis or the Soviet regimes spontaneously come as animal metaphors: cunning, clever, smashing with a paw. Such regimes amputate man's spirit. On the other hand, images for the capitalistic system spontaneously come as machines, or robots, or devouring assembly lines. In America, it is so customary to dismiss human considerations with the phrase "Business is business," that we do not link this phrase with the general inhumanity of the age in which we live. Capitalism deprives a man of his humanity by degrees rather than by violence. Ours is, East or West, not an age favorable to the development of persons.

Moreover, the prominent philosophies of England and America do not do justice to the values by which the best among us live. Neither positivism nor pragmatism give us intellectually defensible grounds for holding the individual human person inviolable, for cherishing compassion for one another, for valuing creativity or love, for esteeming knowledge and research apart from their usefulness, for favoring the asceticism by which individual courage and perseverance are achieved. Neither do they come to grips with the life of personal consciousness we experience, nor with our struggle to come to know ourselves. Many individual men in our culture live according to these values; it is difficult to ascertain by what philosophical justification they do so. It is not surprising that men in other cultures are confused by the contradictions they see in our lives and our theories.

What is man? That is the question around which a culture is organized. If Americans are confused about their identity and destiny, and cannot communicate to other peoples what they seek, it is largely because they no longer have a coherent or consistent answer to this question, nor a vocabulary for expressing it. As a pluralistic people, they do not have and do not wish to have a vision of man which could be made over into an orthodoxy. But they do not even seem to have an open vision, emphasizing those powers all of them can share in living a harmonious, developing national life—the powers of insight and commitment to the unrestricted drive to understand. It is these powers, precisely because they do not limit or restrict man to a definite image, but encourage the pursuit of self-discovery and openness and revision, which are most universal to men. It is these powers which have resonance in the hearts of all men, and which make of Americans members of the human race. It is the liberating of these powers which made the American revolution a great spiritual victory for the entire world.

What is man? Neither positivism nor idealism account for the human experience. The task of working out a pattern of vision capable of accounting for the contrarieties and tensions of the human experience is one of the most important conditions for the renewal of civilization. For reasons often suggested in this book, the experience of understanding or insight seems to be the most central human experience, and the most basic as a starting place for working out that pattern of vision. The search for clarity, the quest for certainty, seem to be fundamentally misdirected. Understanding is primary; when we understand perfectly, clarity and certainty follow. The more we search for the latter, the smaller and smaller grows the circle of human experience in which our search can succeed; the Cartesian reconstruction normally ends in skepticism. On the other hand, the more we pursue understanding, the greater become our chances of attaining clarity and certainty too.

It is a first step even to see that there are at least three patterns for the mind, to see how each differs in one's own experience, and to be able to move from one to another. The peculiarity of "patterns of vision" is that the same facts or the same logical argument may be evaluated differently by men in each pattern; the "pattern" is characterized by the habits and attitudes which lead a man to value certain facts or certain kinds of argument over others. Only rarely can one settle an argument between men in different patterns by appealing to a set of facts or by laying out the propositions of the argument in logical form. Rather, the men in conflict seem to "miss" one another; they argue at cross-purposes; they generally do not even understand each other, for they are looking for different aspects, and have different criteria for what shall count as evidence. Nothing is so common in human experience as this kind of disagreement; yet nothing has received less adequate attention from philosophers. Attention to language and logic, though more common, is less near the heart of the matter.

One of the advantages in choosing understanding as one's starting place in coming to grips with human experience is that understanding is a dynamic activity; from the time of our first insights, we are always learning. An active intelligence always has more questions and is not satisfied until all questions are answered. Morality, science, and practical efficiency all depend on such intelligence. So, in another way, do love, art, and sympathy. If we place our central emphasis on the demands and limits of human understanding, it is unlikely that we will confuse term with process, utopias with the real world, eschatology with history. We will be satisfied with the intelligibility that is at present possible, and look forward to development and revision. We will not expect men to come perfect like Venus full-blown from the sea, nor for institutions to be wholly rational or completely realized in history.

Another advantage to singling out the experience of insight is that it enables us to differentiate the three patterns of vision. The first pattern, that of expedience, favors "facts;" it favors sense observation. The second pattern, idealism, favors insight or intuition; it favors the intuitive grasp of possibility or form in the data. It favors *possibility*, for we can conceive of anything; and it prefers its conceptions to the present facts. This is why the second pattern is utopian. The third pattern of vision, on the other hand, recognizes the claims of the other two; it reflects upon these claims; it estimates the degree to which the facts prized by the one support the intuitions prized by the other. After reflection, it affirms as worthy of belief just those insights which are justified by the facts. What characterizes the third pattern is reflection. In reflection, a man draws on all his resources: his past experiences, habits of judgment, stock of information, accumulated insights. He as it were takes possession of himself and commits himself to the affirmation or denial which he makes. The whole person is engaged in this third pattern of vision. That is why it needs a personalistic philosophy to create a vocabulary by which to express it, and why until our time these issues have been difficult to speak about.

Corresponding to each of the three patterns of vision, we may roughly distinguish awareness of phenomena, intelligible unity, and existence or truth. Accordingly, we may also distinguish the demands of expedience, utopia, and the actual historical situation. With these distinctions, we may criticize a pragmatic politician like President Kennedy, according as his pragmatism inclines more toward the first

or toward the third pattern. The temptation of the pragmatist is to take the short-range view and be too subservient to immediate facts; the demands of the third pattern
are not utopian but pragmatic, yet take into account the
claims of the utopian pattern. In rhetoric, Mr. Kennedy
inclines to the hard-headed but inspiring third pattern; in
action, he inclines to the short-range considerations and intellectual timidity of the first pattern. Mr. Eisenhower
inclined to the platitudes of "the American way of life,"
a utopia in the past, the second pattern, while drifting with
the currents of history as though he lived in the first pattern.
The clearest (though not the only) difference between Mr.
Kennedy and Mr. Eisenhower, therefore, is in their rhetoric; but even that is sufficient to have changed the mood of
the country.

   In the traditional language of philosophy, the third pattern of vision does not incline a man to look for some
mysterious radiation from "being" by which he will be
affected, nor to look for some static "form" in things. It
does not lead him on a quest for being, naively understood.
It leads him to seek answers for his questioning intelligence.
(In Aristotle, the names for the four causes and for most
of the categories are derived from the relevant interrogative
pronoun, adjective, or adverb; the asking of questions is
central to the Aristotelian epistemology.) The language
of "being" and "form" can be most misleading unless they
are translated back into the language of inquiring intelligence, from which they originally derived.

   Finally, the third pattern of vision cannot live in schools,

only in persons. In the schools, one can master a whole
system of definitions, but in the wrong pattern of vision, or
without the ability to distinguish the patterns. Thus arise
the vices of the academicians, who know all the words but
do not come to grips with the reality. Any institution which
favors a single system of philosophy is in danger of misleading its students, by not giving them experience in other
ways of thought and patterns of vision.

How is the third pattern of vision related to faith? What
makes it a *Christian* empiricism? In the first place, "natural"
and "supernatural" are abstractions; there is only one concrete historical world. Christianity claims to be the fullness
of human nature—*anima naturaliter Christiana*—but it
does not claim to be the one camp to which by natural
process all men must automatically or forcibly belong. Attempts to force anyone's conscience are radically evil; the
history of Christianity, like that of other world religions,
is too scarred by this ancient, misdirected form of zeal.
Christianity claims to be open to all men; to oblige all men
by the profoundest depths of their nature; to touch all men
with the call to rejuvenate themselves and to surpass themselves by entering into communion with their God, a Person, whose whole nature is insight and love. Christianity
claims that at the core of the universe is personal communication and love, not silence or irrationality. But Christian
as well as unbeliever is deprived of sight, hearing, and even
feeling in the effort to check this claim. Both, moreover,
face the evils of life equally.

The freedom with which men receive this call in their

hearts and respond to it necessitates, in creatures who can fail, the existence of two camps, two cities. There must be, and there always are, those who hear and accept, and those who for one reason or another do not. That there are two cities is no mystery to those who know what faith and freedom are. To those who do not trust freedom and prefer some artificial substitute to faith, this division is a source of scandal. They feel more secure in their own faith if it does not seem to be free but thrust upon them and protected by closed ranks. On the other hand, some nonbelievers appear to make faith seem like an emotional leap, so that they will not be faced with a serious intellectual decision.

Thus to some nonbelievers the historic Church may seem a revelation which contradicts the revelation of Christ, and they will quote. "By their fruits you will know them." They will point out, with Sidney Hook, that Catholic countries are notably easy prey to communism; that Catholic Austria and Germany could not prevent the rise of Hitler, or the murdering of the Jews; that in countless ways the moral consciousness of believers has seemed especially obtuse or apathetic. But then there are two things which interfere with one's judging of the fruits: one's pattern of vision, and one's looking for the wrong fruits. The fruits of Christianity are deceptive. The Christian revolution is a quiet revolution; its greatest achievements are inner; its deepest life is hidden in God. St. Augustine perhaps more than any other Christian was tortured over this hiddenness and paucity of true believers: how much chaff, how little wheat are on the area-floor; how large each grain of chaff, how small the wheat. Externally, Christ has turned proportions upside-down. If Sidney Hook, for example, were a Christian, undoubtedly he would be one of the earnest ones, grievously wounded like Augustine by the sight of those who failed, but faithful to his own belief nonetheless. Standing in rank does not make the Christian; were all others to be unfaithful, still, the man who believes must hold to faith. It would be dishonest to cease to believe because many, most, or all Christians fail; dishonest, too, not to accept belief for that kind of reason. (In Mr. Hook's case, there are other reasons, some of them apparently due to his views on the nature of philosophy.)

The great stumbling block for many who do not believe is their unexpressed desire for a perfect Church, fully interior, giving clear guidance in every moral dilemma, defending all the values dear to man's personal, social, and political life, each in its due season. An imperfect Church arouses their incredulity. It would be beautiful to have a Church not touched by history, an efficient way of guaranteeing the production of many practical saints, a Church as exhilarating as mathematics, a Church as ordered, peaceful, and sensible as the life of a professor. But men, even under cassocks, are unreliable; the world has no order, peace, or sense to spare. The Church embedded like a seed into history is not beautiful. Often, the bureaucrats gain control of it. Often, the lineaments of Christ are not easy to detect in it. One believes, one does not see.

On the other hand, the nonbeliever does not always notice the contradictions in his own pattern of vision. Claiming that life is meaningless, he often lives according to the very laws of consciousness which lead believers to affirm that it is meaningful. He says life is impersonal, yet he loves. He sees that politics is power, yet struggles for political morality. He claims there is no such thing as truth, yet asks academic freedom to pursue it. He fails to see why being should be considered of any higher value than non-being, yet cherishes creativity as the way to self-fulfillment. He fails to see the coherence between scientific and moral striving and the Christian conception of a God who is the light of truth: discovered in the world through the unity of science, discovered in man's heart through fidelity to self: God closer to us than we to ourselves. The nonbeliever is faithful to his conscience, faithful to the "polar light" he feels within; like Camus he delights in honesty. But isn't that the light "made in the image of God," the light refracted from "Light inaccessible?" He does not notice that he cannot deny this God save by this light: deny in words while sharing the reality.

Until the nonbeliever sees the ambivalences in his own shifts from nihilism to joy in human consciousness, he cannot ask the right questions for reaching belief. Until the nonbeliever decides whether he is seeking a perfect or imperfect Church, he cannot be sure to recognize Christ's mustard seed. The reflective pattern of vision, neither positivistic nor utopian, offers the best prospects of recognition.

Even so, not every one will see. God grants to whom He will, and not the worthiest.

Even the believer will best understand the Church only if he moves beyond the first two patterns of vision. The Church is a continuing revelation; its presence is a continuous "sign raised up for the nations," as the First Vatican Council said. But here too one's pattern of vision dictates what one sees. Approach with the pattern of what could be or should be, and one envisages all sorts of programs that begin: "If only Catholics would . . ." and that promise then a pleasing image. But will such programs tell us what the Church exists to say? Will these programs give us revelation? It seems rather there will be always something false in them. They give us a utopian Christianity, an image where there is a good deal more perfection than we now know. Such perfection on earth or otherworldliness does not seem to be the meaning of the Church. For what of periods of little zeal, of little idealism? The apologist is forced to run breathlessly from one battlefield to another, trying to give the right image of the Church where his fellow Catholics have given the uninspiring image. And bitterness dogs many ardent believers for no other reason: they cannot keep up.

Approach, on the other hand, with the pattern of vision of the expedient mind, and one sees little wrong with the present or historic image of the Church. After all, most men are slaves of passion or prejudice; they'd criticize the Church and the clergy whatever is done. One tends then to

see the Church as an external society like all external societies—like the Republic of Venice or the Kingdom of
France. This is not inaccurate, in a way; but the images and
the unconscious attitudes it conjures up cry for comparison
with the Gospels. One tends to look at buildings, at pres-
sure-power, at crowds, at numbers of Communions—at
"facts"—to buttress one's security. What results is a boast-
ing of the "glories" of the Church: of Crusades and
Canonized Saints and Kingdoms swayed and Catholic
Generals saying Science Not Enough. The expedient mind
has no choice but to produce favorable facts, and to be
blind to disturbing facts, for the sake of its peace. The
experience of seeing a man possessed in unconscious moments of such externalism and saying pious things at other
moments—all obviously in blissful ignorance of his in-
consistencies—is all too frequent in dealing with a certain
kind of ecclesiastical mind.

What then is the Church? God became man; that is
the first revelation about our existence. Christ is committed
to history. He is open to failure and utter degradation:
"Ugly and, as it were, despised and the most abject of men."
(Is. 53). Neither the utopian nor the man of expedience
can grasp this nettle. For given to the more or less unintelligible flux of possibilities is now God's Son; God ratifies the
creation He has made by accepting it as it is for His Son
too. Further, He accepts the unintelligibility thrown into
history by unreason and malice; Christ is given to the
mercy of these too, and of course there is no mercy. The

Sanhedrin finds it expedient that a strong and innocent man die. Pilate finds no guilt but condemns. Enemies made over the months crush Him. And He dies seeing nothing done, nothing a success. The resurrection comes to complete the mystery, but it is *afterward*. Most of all, for our purposes, it is incomplete so far as the members of Christ go, so far as the Church goes. It is done, we are already with Christ in God, the battle is already won—but only in faith, not to our eyes. This, I think, is the mystery of the cross, "The sign raised up among the nations."

The Church, too, is this sign. The Church is this same revelation continued. So it is that the Church suffers and is disfigured, is betrayed and grows weary, has no energy and falls almost to death. What God is revealing to us again and again is the mystery of our existence: life is like this. Natural laws are not suspended. Unintelligible malice reaps its due fruit of complication and absurdity in society. Weakness and failure and betrayal mature into disaster. Scandal and blindness and hardness grow swiftly where their seeds fall; good seed dies where the soil is thin. But under this all, as under the disfigured Christ, is the Son of God. This is what revelation asks of us. Our existence is an imprisonment, and redemption is not utopian freedom but freedom that suffers. One must *stay in* the world. One must stay in expedience and blind power and the play of unknown possibilities. On the other hand, into unintelligibility comes the Light; among imponderables, threads the Way; into what would be worse than death comes the

Life. Faith asks this of us. But faith cannot ask even this if we do not exorcise ourselves of patterns of vision incompatible with its acceptance, or its maturation in full, blooming Christian life.

Thus believers need not plan "if only. . . ." We need not wait until Catholics come to fuller knowledge of their faith, or live it more fully, and thus lend to the Church its "true" external image. We could do no better than humbly admit what we are, preach it even on the housetops, our disfigurements in Christ as well as our beauty in Him. For the revelation God is giving through the Church is not finished beauty or perfection; it is beauty-in-process, it is beauty often wasted or twisted or abominated. But often, too, reaching its term, its hidden term. The sight of one of these rare lives living by the Gospels is worth more than all the rest of life. God, at least, seems to view the world that way.

POSTSCRIPT

A great future awaits America, and Catholicism in America. But everything depends on the prophets seizing leadership from the hands of the bureaucrats. "I have not come to bring peace, but the sword." The fruit of the Lord's presence is not apathy, nor is it regularity and order. It is the desire for justice; it is compassion for the suffering. When Catholics come alive in America, the moral revolution Charles Péguy wrote about will be one step more advanced. The entire race will feel the difference.

The future depends on the young, who do not wait for their elders; the world their elders leave them is not admirable. The young need to ask advice and to learn; to be rash is no advantage. But they must be freer than their elders were. They must return to the traditions of the Gospels and the early Church. They must take risks, and set new precedents. They must not be afraid of trying what has never been tried before; otherwise, they shall never be creative. They must not be afraid of authority. Youth, not authority, is the source of creativity. The young must be proud, bold, and free if they wish to create. When, finally, authority intervenes, as it too often and too quickly does in our generation, it is ordinarily more noble to obey than to disobey; and to obey with love, even if one feels that right is on one's side, and even if authority has been employed unfairly. Halted in one direction, the energy of the Gospels seeks out another crevice for its growth. The mustard seed, finally, breaks its pots—patience is on the side of the Lord. Those motivated by self-love give up.

I cannot hold back one final note. The young Negro in America who, against apathy and brutality, calmly, with dignity, with peace, began in the Spring of 1963 to seek no more than his right to be taken as a man, is creating one of the most beautiful testaments in the history of our land. He deserves our companionship, however ugly the struggle becomes. We are living in a century of blood and heroism. If ever some among us desired to live in a time when we might give our lives to justice, ours is such a time. Let us hope that many from among young Catholics join with their brothers, join the few, who work always and everywhere for justice.

ACKNOWLEDGMENTS

The author wishes to thank the editors of the following weeklies, monthlies, and quarterlies, in whose pages some of the material for this book first appeared, and by whose permission it has here been used: *Christian Century* for Chapter 5; *The Commonweal* for Chapters 6, 9, 10, and 12–15; *Harper's Magazine* for Chapter 8; *motive magazine* for Chapter 1; *The Nation* for Chapter 7; *The New Republic* for Chapters 2 and 11; *Perspectives* for Chapter 4; and *Review for Religious* for Chapter 3.